Find Yourself at Home

FIND YOURSELF
AT HOME

A CONSCIOUS APPROACH to SHAPING YOUR SPACE and YOUR LIFE

EMILY GROSVENOR

CHRONICLE PRISM

Library of Congress Cataloging-in-Publication Data available.

ISBN 978-1-7972-2140-3

Manufactured in China.

Design by Domino Design.
Typesetting by Happenstance Type-O-Rama.
Typeset in Verlag and Freight Text.
Essential Feng Shui is a registered trademark of Western School of Feng Shui.

10 9 8 7 6 5 4 3 2 1

Chronicle books and gifts are available at special quantity discounts to corporations, professional associations, literacy programs, and other organizations. For details and discount information, please contact our premiums department at corporatesales@chroniclebooks.com or at 1-800-759-0190.

CHRONICLE PRISM

Chronicle Prism is an imprint of Chronicle Books LLC, 680 Second Street, San Francisco, California 94107
www.chronicleprism.com

To my mother, Susan Grosvenor,
who taught me how to love the life I choose.

CONTENTS

PHILOSOPHY

Connect with the Mystery and Power of Your Home

SPACE

Prepare Your Environment for Your Story

BUILD

Discover Design Tools to Cue Your Behavior

DESIRE

Bring Your Aspirations into Your Space

DESTINY

Take Your Purpose into the World

INTRODUCTION

About a decade ago, when I walked through the front door of the house where I live today for the first time, I didn't see any rainbows cresting above its roof. My husband, Adam, and I had never bought a home before, and I was on a one-day blitz of twelve house tours in a small town. This house was just a normal, suburban family home scrubbed clean of every mark of its previous occupants and staged for sale. But I already knew enough about houses to intuit how we might turn it into a magical collaborator in our lives. It had a feeling of just enough: space, light, flow, rooms, and backyard. And most importantly in my estimation, it had a corner bathtub illuminated by two windows.

I knew this could be our home because I had been training for this moment my entire life.

I grew up a dreamy, discerning kid in the middle of Amish country in a suburb of Lancaster, Pennsylvania, which is often lauded as one of the best places to live in the United States. On the weekends, while other families carted themselves off to church and Sunday school and services, my sister Ashley and I would gather with Mom in bed, where she was already blanketed by the real estate section of the *Lancaster New Era*. Ashley and I read the comics while Mom pored over the open houses. Then, mostly just for fun, we'd spend part of an afternoon touring houses for sale. I always thought we were moving, but we were really doing it to dream. Even today, Sunday from 1 to 4 p.m. holds an enchanting air of possibility to me.

During the 1990s, Lancaster was an Open House Paradise, with unending historic properties for sale and a spate of new housing developments. We toured both recent construction and historic properties dating as far back as Revolutionary America. My mother preferred visiting new constructions, since she has always loved fresh starts. She loved the architecture of older homes but often bristled at other people's style. It makes sense to me now—once you know yourself and your taste, a blank slate leaves room for your own fingerprints. She could tell the moment she walked in whether she liked a home—she has a thing for foyers. I had bedroom eyes. I went upstairs first, usually by myself, to pick out a room to occupy with my dreaming. My only burning question was: Who would I be if I lived in this house?

I have always preferred homes heavy on story—still do. Empty rooms rarely tell much of a tale. Out of the hundreds of open houses we visited, the ones I remember most are those that were still alive with the energies of their previous occupants, where I could imagine the exact people who had lived there. The 1950s cottage with the original black-and-white-checked flooring. The '80s contemporary stuffed— ha!—with taxidermy, including a full-size ostrich. The house with the Hollywood bathroom lights and shag carpet. The incongruent opulence of a McMansion owned by a church pastor.

Nevertheless, each time we returned from these visits to our own Cape Cod–styled cottage, Mom cut the engine, sighed, regarded our

home, and said: "I'll take that one." I think about that moment often—how she chose our own life, again and again.

After I left my childhood home, while I spent a decade cycling through more than a dozen temporary homes, I visited storied homes whenever I could. This taught me a lot about the relationship between people and their spaces. I lived in concrete student housing blocks while touring the megalomaniacal castles of Europe. In three years, I moved through three apartments in three neighborhoods in Washington, DC, visiting our nation's illustrious halls of power on weekends but also jetting off to places like Washington's home Mt. Vernon, Dumbarton Oaks, Tudor Place, and the Woodrow Wilson House.

After we were married, Adam and I kept moving and visiting famous homes (he is quite obliging). We stayed in a condo as we toured the Mount, Edith Wharton's home, on our honeymoon (seriously, he's a saint). During Iowa's winters, we froze in student housing and posed in front of the tiny white cottage that inspired Grant Wood's *American Gothic*. After moving to Oregon, we moved in quick succession—from a brand-new apartment block to a 1910 farmhouse to a 1940s cottage. On weekends, we visited Timberline, the lodge that served as the exterior for the hotel in *The Shining*, or we lurked about the Gordon House, a Frank Lloyd Wright Usonian home.

Finally, during the worst housing market crisis in American history, we bought a house. To make it our home, though, I knew I had to incorporate all the lessons I had learned ever since those first open house tours. First, I nested like a beast. I learned to see decorating as a form of visual storytelling, where color, form, negative space, and objects interact to tell a cohesive story. Once we had kids, I experimented with how different layouts and visual cues affected their behavior and my own, all the while asking myself what changes we could make in order to live more harmoniously together. Adam and I had the classic newlywed face-offs about interior style, but we found ways to accommodate each other and to create a shared aesthetic that went beyond what either of us individually imagined. After about five years, I began to see our home as my own personal energy vortex, an oracle site—a living, pulsing place to reflect on our lives, shape our stories, and renew our strength. To me, our home wasn't meant to be a sanctuary, a place to hide away from the outside world. Instead, it became a place to embody our family's deepest values and remind us of who we could be in the world.

Professionally, I became a magazine editor in the home-and-garden space, writing stories about people changing their lives through home design. I love the aspirational world of magazines, and that work is what I still do. But to me, these stories of transformation are not just rote before-and-afters. My editorial eye is drawn to how people use their spaces to support their transitions, and how, in turn, the spaces we live in shape our lives.

So I also began studying the ancient philosophies of energy and space, and I got a certificate in Essential Feng Shui,® a school of the ancient art informed by Western living. Now I also work with people directly to help them design their homes to support and shift their lives.

All my life, I have been studying houses and how they impact us. In my own life and in my work with others, I have witnessed downright magical shifts occur simply by redesigning living spaces. These experiences lend credence to what ancient masters have known for centuries and what modern environmental psychologists now confirm: Our spaces affect us profoundly, whether we are paying attention or not.

PHILOSOPHY

CONNECT WITH THE MYSTERY AND POWER OF YOUR HOME

1

THE **INFINITE POSSIBILITIES** OF **HOME**

Your home is the center of your world. It is a place of specific, wise energy that welcomes you after the long journey of your day into a lush setting of ritual and messaging, deep reflection and dreaming, gathering and exchange, letting go and trusting something outside of yourself. Home is a place of great power and purpose—as sacred a location as any major historic setting or pilgrimage site. When you shape it consciously, it shapes you back.

When you see your home like this—not just as a shelter or a safe space but as an essential collaborator in your life—everything changes. Mundane tasks become magical. Any adjustments you make to your rooms, big and small, carry an air of personal transformation. To paint the walls becomes a radical, spiritual act. Switching up decorative objects creates nothing less than inner transformation. Even walking through the front door feels like arriving at a destination of profound significance. The more you interact with your space with curiosity, reverence, and a spirit of collaboration, the more you will feel "at home"—both enjoying and in love with your own life.

The Empowering, Transformational Home

Most people consider home to be a place of comfort and safety. This has never been more true than during the ongoing COVID-19 pandemic, particularly during the period when schools and companies shifted almost entirely to remote learning and work. Suddenly, without warning or preparation, our homes became shelters that had to support all our needs. This shift forced us to reconsider what our homes mean to us—and how they might need to continue changing to support us in the face of future challenges, including climate change. All in all, these events have reminded us of the power of places. We can no longer treat our homes as pretty boxes to disappear into. To live our best lives, we must reenvision our homes as empowering environments that embody who we are and aspire to be and that support every aspect of our lives.

When home is a place of empowerment, it becomes a playground to explore our ideas of self, a message board that cues us to aspirational goals, and a story where we choose which parts of our past to let go of and which to carry forward. In addition to meeting our basic needs for shelter, our homes can also fulfill our needs for serenity, creativity, meaning, and purpose. Our homes hold infinite possibilities. They aren't just places to keep our stuff. They can be living, evolving embodiments of the story we choose to live.

This book details the methods I use in my own home and with clients to create transformational environments that shape identity, behavior, and purpose. I developed these ideas and approaches during my years working as a design journalist and as a private consultant and from a lifetime of "reading the room," which began during those house tours of my youth. Throughout, I include my own stories about the incredible impact of collaborative spaces as well as the stories of the people I've worked with. I feel immensely lucky to be able to share these tales, and I've sought to present people who represent a wide range of backgrounds and beliefs (while changing names and identifying details to preserve privacy). My hope is that, with this advice and these examples, you can discover how to create your own collaborative home space for yourself.

Becoming Conscious of Space

In order to transform your home into a great collaborator in your life, you must first become conscious of how your space affects you and approach any changes with deep awareness. This means moving beyond questions of function and aesthetics to assessing your space at the level of energy and overall feel and by learning some of the tenets of environmental psychology and feng shui. Becoming conscious about your home means developing a lifestyle that supports the person you want to be and making design decisions aligned with your big-picture vision of life.

Becoming conscious means noticing what is and is not working and then sitting thoughtfully with possible design solutions that could change the atmosphere. This has nothing to do with buying luxurious, expensive furnishings or trying to emulate a space that belongs to someone else. It doesn't necessarily require massive, full-on makeovers or rebuilding portions of your home. It's not about following of-the-moment trends or styles to impress the masses on Instagram. It also doesn't mean scrolling online shops until your eyes go blurry.

Instead, it means giving yourself the luxury of self-reflection and the time to feel the effects of the changes you are making. Often, it means working first with what you have, such as by rearranging spaces to increase energy, ease, and happiness. It means evaluating changes for how well they enrich human environments, not necessarily whether the décor fulfills a certain style. Becoming conscious of how spaces affect you is a slow dance over time: As you consciously transform your home, your rooms will hum with their own essence and vibrancy.

Some people are already energetically open. They have a natural ability to feel and shape a space. They can tell immediately and intuitively whether walking into a room feels welcoming and harmonious or off-putting and disjointed. But anyone can learn how to notice, direct, and shape the energies within a room. And anyone can find it hard to evaluate their own home, or they can get bogged down and overwhelmed by the unending options available in the market. Whatever is true for you, and whenever you hit a stumbling block in this process, be gentle with yourself. By consciously developing a thoughtful approach to shaping your home, your skills and confidence will steadily improve.

Change Your Environment, Change Yourself

We are creatures existing in place, characters informed by our settings, so it follows that changing our environment will impact who we are. You may have already experienced the life-changing moment when shifting something within your home shifts something within you. A big or small alteration, especially anything that brings more beauty, function, and flow to a space, inspires a sense of ease and delight. The spirit exalts, the heart rejoices. The nerves settle, the soul sinks in.

The more we align our home with the person we want to be, the more our home becomes our essential collaborator: a place of mysterious power and messaging that can send us back into the world with strength and purpose.

Through the way we design our home, we can gain a sense of power and confidence that nudges us toward our goals and inspires the activities, feelings, and social interactions we desire. The more we experiment with placement, color, materiality, and other design tools, the more we find ourselves "at home"—that elusive feeling of serenity and arrival.

This sense of harmony is the premise of feng shui and dovetails nicely with the field of environmental psychology, both of which I've studied with great interest. I will never tire of trying to understand the mechanisms behind how space affects us. Each year, research by environmental psychologists unearths new insights—whether the effect of clutter on our mental states (it's bad, no surprise there), how an office setup affects what people accomplish in the workplace, or more evidence of the never-ending benefits of our connection to the natural world.

That said, intuition is our most powerful compass and friend. We don't need to read a bunch of empirical studies to discover for ourselves how our own settings influence us. Nor, as one of my feng shui mentors once told me, do we have to know or care how energy work actually functions in order for it to work. Some people want to run for the hills when they hear talk about "energy" and "vibrations," but they can still follow their own inner voice, aesthetic sense, and sense of self to improve their home. My approach is to blend the emerging science of environmental psychology with the ancient practices of feng shui to make home-shaping a pursuit anyone can feel comfortable practicing and have success with.

Be Prepared for Change

By shifting the energy of our home, we are inviting change, but that can still be difficult. Further, we can't control the results (wouldn't that be nice!). Energy work for the home can be unpredictable—that's part of its charm—and so we have to respond to what life throws at us with ingenuity and adaptability. For instance, we might create a family altar hoping to repair a relationship with an aunt, but we find our interactions with our brother start to flourish instead. We might ask for more respect in our current job and end up getting another offer entirely out of thin air. Shifting energy always seems to work in our favor, or achieve something positive, but outcomes aren't always what we imagined. There is rarely a straight line from before to after.

Though the outcomes of energy work cannot be predicted, our intentions when shifting energy matter. When I go into a client's home, I take a good look at what's going on in the environment (what I call "reading the room"), and then I make suggestions for changes based on what I know about the client's story and their current struggles. My own sense of style and the specifics of what *I* would do are unimportant. I'm just an idea person helping someone meet and overcome their problems by suggesting possible design solutions that might shift things for them.

I've seen amazing results with home energy work. I've had clients get new jobs out of the blue and start partnerships after a long romantic dry spell. I've also seen difficult, decades-long relationships end after spatial changes were made. I've helped small-business owners attract new customers by reworking the entrance to their offices, and I've helped a homeless shelter shape the behavior of young people coming in off the streets. Once, after an older woman finally redid the bedroom in a home she had lived in for forty years, she abruptly moved eight states away in order to start over. Did the new bed, carpet, and paint cause it to happen? Of course not. Did the changes spark a necessary identity shift that allowed her to take one of the biggest leaps in her life? Perhaps.

One thing has become clear to me as I've explored how making mindful shifts within home spaces supports humans. Taking any action at all within the home—whether it's cleaning up a messy counter or painting a wall or just moving around objects—may feel like a quiet response to dealing with the constantly changing world outside, but it is also a potent one. Staying limber at home and enjoying the process helps us adjust at the soul level to the challenges of whatever is happening outside our walls.

THE FIVE STEPS OF
FINDING YOURSELF AT HOME

My goal is to provide you with the tools to make any place you live, any space, feel like "home." This is a feeling you can cultivate whenever you want or need to. By applying the tenets of environmental psychology and by noticing and respecting your intuition for what feels authentic and resonant, you can use décor and spatial design to cultivate a more meaningful life. In that sense, I hope you approach reading this book as a way to give yourself permission to prioritize the big picture of your life.

I have divided the process into five steps (which align with the book's five parts), but these are not meant as a list of prescribed tasks you must accomplish. There is no single "right way" to turn your home into an essential collaborator in your life. Everyone's situation is different, and whatever the current state of your house, it is already collaborating with you.

Through these five steps, I will show you how to use the tenets of design, object placement, environmental psychology, and storytelling to foster an empowering conversation with your living space. Not every suggestion may work in your space or for who you are and what you want. While some suggestions can involve spending money, nothing *requires* you to spend money; this process can be successful with any budget. You get to decide which ideas to pursue and how to pursue them.

Step 1. Connect with the mystery and power of your home

Train yourself to see your home as a place entwined with your own energy and story. Reimagine your home as a partner in all you do.

Step 2. Prepare your environment for your story

Set the stage for shaping your story at home. Clear your environment of past energies and set your intentions for your space based on the person you'd like to become.

Step 3. Discover design tools to cue your behavior

Take simple actions to send yourself desired messages in your space. Create a color story, use visual cues, incorporate primal urges like scent and animal symbology, and adjust the space where you do your most important work.

Step 4. Bring your aspirations into your space

Using a feng shui–based home energy map, connect your home's layout to your personal aspirations. Using this, you can make intentional changes in different areas of the home to produce shifts in confidence, type of energy, and openness to change.

Step 5. Take your purpose into the world

Discover ways to ask for what you want and put your mission out in the world.

How to Deepen Your Practice

Finally, at the end of each chapter, I've included reflective questions to help you deepen your understanding and awareness of both your space and yourself. Think of these "Find Yourself" sections as conversation starters between you and your space. Each chapter's questions and exercises can help you reenvision your home and foster your collaborative relationship with it.

Throughout this book, proceed gently and give yourself time as you align your home to suit your purpose and your path. Remember, making your space into your home is an ongoing process. Your relationship with your home is one great, long, continuous conversation.

FIND YOURSELF

When was the last time you felt at home?

What do you see your home as: home base? A playground?
A jewel box? Choose a metaphor that captures the
role you want your desired home space to occupy, and
write it down somewhere you can see it every day.

2

PEOPLE SHAPE SPACES, SPACES SHAPE PEOPLE

Since the earliest humans, who sought shelter in caves and used fire for warmth, for cooking, and to connect with the spirit world, people have lived in relationship with the places they inhabit. The formal study of how people interact with space may be somewhat new—the field of environmental psychology has only been around since the 1950s—but people have always existed in a playful feedback loop with their environment. We alter shelters to suit our needs and desires—and we are in turn altered by these spaces.

Today, our homes are a constantly evolving reflection of what is going on within us. They change as we change, moving through the seasons of the year and the stages of our lives. As Winston Churchill put it, in what has become a favorite saying for architects and designers: "We shape our buildings. In turn, our buildings shape us."

Spaces Cue Behaviors

A house is not a home until a human claims it and makes it theirs. Of course, we need spaces to fulfill certain specific, practical functions, but homes also influence our emotions, identity, healing, life purpose, sense of beauty—you name it. Everything we add and take away has an effect; some effects are intended and desired, some undesired. Each choice impacts the overall vibe of the whole.

Our homes contain rich visual and sensual design metaphors that cue our primal human selves. These help us foster states of being, tell our stories, and create meaning. The first step toward creating an empowering environment is identifying and employing these cues consciously and intentionally.

Everything in the home matters. Elements such as architectural structures, appliances, lighting, furniture, décor, and materials can cue certain behaviors and states of being. Architects call these elements "primes," which are any feature that stimulates a response. A doorway, for example, primes us to walk between two spaces; a sink primes us to wash our hands or get a drink. I think the word *prime* sounds too much like math, or a certain online retail behemoth, and so I call them *cues*.

A cue can be employed consciously, but its impact will eventually go unnoticed and become subconscious. We might choose a velvet-covered couch because we want our living room to feel luxurious and comfortable—but over time, our response to the cue can become automatic. We may paint our bedroom blue because blue has been shown to have a soporific effect, but soon enough, we no longer think about how the color helps lull us to sleep—it just does.[1] We install a full-spectrum lightbulb in our home office to keep us awake and on task, but before long, we are just turning on the light. Whether we notice it or not, however, everything we live with has impact. How we design our homes cues certain behaviors and responses, so by choosing which messages are most beneficial, we can nudge ourselves toward a desired outcome.

One reason to be more conscious about how we design our spaces is because of our relative state of unconsciousness most of the time. As much as 95 percent of our thoughts are unconscious.[2] Thus, it's safe to say that if we don't make an effort to shape our space to create our desired states of being, it will keep shaping us, but in a way that is less than optimal. If we want our homes to support our whole selves, we have to spend time and energy creating that.

This means paying attention to every aspect of our home spaces. Rooms are multisensory experiences. Our feet feel the floor and how flooring changes from room to room. Each window provides a different view (and a lack of windows, no view at all). A room with only shared seating might foster more togetherness, but might feel stifling to introverts. Typically, we barely think about how these things might be influencing us. Yet by figuring out the most pleasing arrangement, we might get close to creating what the Germans call a *Gesamtkunstwerk*—a total work of art where different forms combine to create a cohesive whole.

THE BASIC ELEMENTS THAT
MAKE A GREAT HOME

What makes a great home? And how do we maximize our response
to spaces? Environmental psychologists have answered this question
by noting that satisfying homes have four elements in common: First,
humans feel better in structures with strong structural foundations—that
is, walls and roofs—since these allow us to turn off our anxious brains, and
they give us a feeling of stability. Second, we thrive in environments with
views of the natural world; this allows our brains to rest. Third, we respond
positively to the use of natural materials (as opposed to plastics). And
fourth, we need adequate daylight, which allows our bodies to regulate
our sleep and active states.

Here are two more things to keep in mind.

Prospect and Refuge Spaces

Most rooms have a clearly identified function that invites us to action
or to rest. Environmental psychologists call these *prospect* and *refuge*
spaces. Prospect spaces are devoted to specific activities: Kitchens are
for cooking, offices for paying bills, a workbench for building, and so on.
Refuge spaces like bedrooms, a reading chair, or a bathtub inspire retreat,
rest, introspection, and possibly solitude. Thus, defining the main use of
each space is very important. This also accounts for why modern, mixed-
use spaces can cause so much stress or conflict. A shared multipurpose
room is cueing a variety of behaviors. While having your office in your
bedroom might make practical sense in terms of available space, it will
also make shifting between activity and rest more difficult.

Visual and Sensual Cues

Once the purpose of a space is defined, the next things to consider are its *visual and sensual cues*. In essence, what is a room or space telling you? Most of my work with clients focuses on creating purposeful messaging by adjusting visual and sensual cues. This involves considering what a structure, a piece of furniture, or an object is cueing us to do or to feel, and then readjusting elements and spaces in ways that benefit our whole selves.

FIND YOURSELF

In what ways have you been shaped by the places you have lived in the past?

In what ways is the place you live now actively shaping you?

3

THE SECRET MESSAGES
OF HOME STYLES

T he house I live in now—which my husband and I bought in an Oregon wine country town in 2011—was never conceived to help us make friends. Built in 2005 in a vaguely craftsman style with a front entrance set off by posts made of river rock, it has a bit in common with what's known as a *snout house*—a home where the garage juts out toward the street, obscuring the view of private spaces. Snout houses were largely a response to builders having to contend with the challenges of a smaller lot. Snout houses have something to say. It might be: "Hey, we can all fit in here!" Even though they bring you physically closer to your neighbors, they make for unfriendly streets, with drives lined with garages instead of front doors. In the past decade, city planners in places like Bozeman, Montana, and Portland, Oregon, have even considered whether to ban the extreme versions of these types of homes because they can make the community as a whole feel antisocial.[3]

In 2020, at the start of the COVID-19 pandemic, my husband and I noticed the loneliness of our house's setup, and we started discussing house projects that might help with that then-new thing called social distancing. His mother had recently moved across the country to live near us, and we wanted a safe way to gather with her and with our friends. We settled on adding a front porch that extended from our front door, creating another place to safely hang out.

The porch changed our lives. Since it faced west, it gave our home its first view of the setting sun, which sparked an ongoing ritual of evening gatherings and porch parties. The street's caravan of neighbors soon transformed from strangers with labels like "That Guy with the Dachshund" to actual, named humans we knew. Children from all over made a practice of coming by for a quick chat. Our front porch announced to everyone that we were people open to connection. In a real sense, we chose something we valued—more interaction with people—and changed our home to embody and cultivate that value. Now we have a designated "porch season."

HOUSE HOROSCOPES

In general, architecture embodies what society values. Buildings give shape to human aspirations and intentions. Think of the cathedrals of Europe: Their interiors inspire spiritual awe while impressing on us how small humans are in the big picture of things. Now consider a prison cell, whose stark barrenness strips us of our humanity and purpose. You could also consider America's Levittown homes of the 1950s—quaint, boxy homes on equally sized patches of earth for newly middle class families.

We know more now about how architecture shapes human beings and vice versa than ever before. We know that the way spaces are designed can either diminish or enhance our well-being, and yet, we tend to choose homes by engaging with what we like, as opposed to what might shape our behavior, our personal missions, and our relationships. When we're considering a home or evaluating our current space, in addition to all the other attributes we're looking for, it's good to examine how a particular house style can influence us and who we long to become.

Here is a list of common house styles and an assessment of the kinds of energies they foster.

A-FRAME

A house shaped like an *A* is an ancient style seen around the world. In the United States, the A-frame cabin became popular in the 1960s and 1970s as a second or DIY vacation home. Newer adjustments to the style can accommodate its drawbacks: It's difficult to decorate sloped walls, and they often lack exterior light except for one glass wall in the back. But there is no mistaking the iconic message of independence and perpetual vacation. They appeal to those for whom "play hard" is more important than "work hard," but they can also feel constrained. Many people build bump-outs, or small additions, to compensate.

CAPE COD

Imagine a storybook home and your mind might summon this 1.5-floor style popularized in New England. Some call it the quintessential American style, as its form, size, and popularity during the twentieth century encapsulates the joys of just enough. Energetically, it's a cozy style, with smaller spaces, pleasing symmetry, and rooms designed to keep people warm during long winters. But Cape Cods can favor private life over public, and they often lack a direct relationship to outdoor spaces.

COLONIAL

All types of colonial architecture recall the mother country where that style originated—hence the terms Dutch colonial, English colonial, and so on. Georgian style in particular, from the era of Kings George II and III, inspired many of the stately homes of the East Coast and those built during the colonial revival of the twentieth century. Think brick facades, white trim, and embellished cornices. People who absolutely *must* have a colonial tend to revere tradition, heritage, and balance. Brick evokes a firm grounding in the world. But beware: Homes that have one of those long front-to-back hallways can make life feel like it is moving too quickly.

COTTAGE

Cottages are physical manifestations of just enough. Other styles can be layered on top of cottages, but our contemporary understanding of cottage style speaks to a love of natural materials, windows and doors, and a welcoming demeanor (we forgive you, Goldilocks). Indeed, comfort and charm reign as the main values of this style. They are good places for folks who don't long to impress the neighbors, but just want to invite them over for tea. This same coziness can be confining, however, and create resistance to change.

CRAFTSMAN

People who feel the craftsman look is their thing tend to be practical, while harboring a quiet rebellion. The craftsman home emerged in response to the ornamentation of the Victorian period; it values the inherent beauty of natural materials and forms above filigree. Lots of variations in craftsman style exist, but most feature elements like low-pitched roofs, exposed beams, and large porches meant to make a home feel cozy, authentic, and warm, with distinct, purpose-suited living spaces. Having everything in its box can be appealing, but too much plainness can dampen individualized expression. To set oneself apart, a little customization in the interior spaces can help.

FARMHOUSE

Farmhouses started dotting the American landscape beginning in the eighteenth century, but today's incarnations have the Sears, Roebuck catalog of the late nineteenth and early twentieth centuries to thank for their ubiquity. Farmhouses exude simple beauty, friendliness (think porches), practicality (clapboard siding), and love of landscape, whether they're part of a farm or not. The farmhouse's modern cousin clearly states that the occupants can be traditional and trend-conscious at the same time. But the style also sends the subtle message that life and work are one and the same.

FRENCH COUNTRY

People who like to have it both ways tend to gravitate toward French country houses, which go all in on mixing rustic and elegant. The style became popular in the United States after World War I. American soldiers returning from France brought with them a love for the beautiful French countryside, where the homes had stone exteriors, sloping roofs, and natural finishes. This soothing, homey style with a bit of bling appeals to those who also not-so-secretly prefer France. Just be aware: Homes built with materials that can't be found locally can sometimes feel at odds with their landscapes, making people feel ill at ease in their setting.

LOG HOME

Rustic finds its high-water mark in the log home—a style that arose in Scandinavia and Eastern Europe, where people literally cut down surrounding forests to build their homes. That's some

major self-determination and dedication embodied by timbers laid horizontally over each other, their gaps filled with mud. Today, log homes come in all kinds of packages to suit various ideals of sustainability, tradition, practicality, and connection to nature. The message they send is rustic solitude, so people who don't like long stretches of time spent alone should steer clear.

MEDITERRANEAN

This style borrows from historic inspirations around the Mediterranean Sea, where red tiled roofs, arched doorways, stucco, and the outdoor lifestyle feel at home. They make most sense in places where that lifestyle is possible—so the Southern and Southwestern states and California. Windows tend to be smaller—who needs all that sunshine— and ornamentation can be great or not much at all. The key here is that you like things sumptuous and sensual, with an easy flow between indoor and outdoor life. Authenticity is key: Placed in the wrong climate, people in Mediterranean-styled homes will feel out of place.

MIDCENTURY MODERN

Showcases for *Mad Men* dreams, midcentury modern homes take their spatial cues from the tenets of the visionary European architects who escaped Nazi Germany before World War II and fled to the United States. They believed form should follow function, so open floor plans valued family togetherness, while large glass windows encouraged people to go outside and connect to the outdoors. Life lived here feels stylish and modern, but as a practical concern, roofs can leak. They aren't ideal for every climate, and have to be adjusted for privacy.

MODERN

No specific silhouette defines the modern home—and that's part of the fun. Modern homes exalt function over ornamentation and hold occupants in a sometimes-cold embrace of concrete, glass, and steel, though smart builders work in some warm wood for comfort. These homes maximize life: what's possible, the view from where we are, the efficiency of structure. They offer a living challenge to think only about what is essential. It's a great style for people who know what they want and have their lifestyle needs dialed in, but it may need some of the hard edges softened.

NEO-ECLECTIC

This isn't really one style unto itself but a combination of styles that emerged as people rejected the flat, boxy, single-floor homes of the midcentury era. It steals and borrows from historic styles to create a whole that feels modern and new, but when done wrong, it can look like it's trying too hard. It speaks of the freedom to choose, to be whatever we want to be, and to create the life that we want for ourselves.

RANCH

Nothing says adaptability like a ranch house. With their long, close-to-the-ground profile, they tell a story of America as it spread out into the suburbs. The ranch style first came into being in the 1920s and had a boom in the 1940s. Ranch houses tend to have features like eat-in kitchens, open concepts, and back patios. People drawn to the ranch might be feeling the need to spread out and take up space in the world while tending to their own basic needs. Like a dream friend, it accommodates many people's energies.

TUDOR

In terms of spaces that embody success, it doesn't get much better than a Tudor, a style borrowed from the half-timbered homes of medieval Europe. They are instantly recognizable for their asymmetrical exteriors adorned with masonry, brickwork, and steep-gabled roofs. There is nothing box-like about them, and interior rooms can be planned out with less thought for maintaining the outside form. Craftsmanship and creativity are high in Tudors, but they can also make you feel like you're living in a rabbit's warren, which may not appeal to those who love symmetry.

VICTORIAN

The much-adorned and adored Victorian style has rooms that really coax people to behave. During the Industrial Revolution, these gorgeous gingerbread homes signaled wealth and status. They had lots of smaller rooms divided up to suit specific purposes and a strong separation between public and private spheres (think large formal entryways and bedrooms tucked away upstairs). Victorians embody life filigreed in all of its fabulosity and a love of boundaries and decorum.

EXERCISE:
DETERMINE YOUR HOME VALUES

In this exercise, assess the values your home currently embodies as well as those you would like it to embody. Your home might reflect needs you no longer have or it might be missing something essential. You might identify emerging priorities you want to invite in or spaces where you can focus more on what is truly important.

Using two pens with different colored ink, make two lists. In one list with one pen, name the qualities that the architecture of your space values. In the second list with the other pen, list the qualities that you'd like your home to value (whether it does currently or not).

Use this sample list of words to get you started and feel free to add your own.

Privacy	Family	Nature
Community	Solitude	Connection
Beauty	Independence	Wellness
Spirituality	Luxury	Education
Creativity	Competition	Curiosity
Serenity	Restoration	Commitment
Cleanliness	Graciousness	Gratitude
Order	Simplicity	Tradition
Openness	Maximalism	Play
Efficiency	Influence	Scholarship
Joy	Grandness	Togetherness
Adventure	Minimalism	Heritage
Scholarship	Stability	Balance

Adjust Your Home to Reflect Your Values

"Home values" refers not to how much your home is worth monetarily. It refers to the values embedded in the design of your home and in the ways you use those spaces. This is a combination of the functionality of the building layout itself and of the ways you carve out places inside its four walls to create meaningful moments for your family. For instance, this might mean the kitchen island where you roll out pies, the window seat where you teach your children to read, the living room corner devoted to your late-night music jam, the wall of portraits where you honor your ancestors.

Evaluate the two lists you made in the exercise to see how well your desired home values align with those your home currently embodies. Then use this exercise to brainstorm possible house projects that add personal value, not resale value. You can weigh the wisdom of any larger house project and its effect on your financial investment in your home, but if you have plans to stay rooted in place or to work on your emotional attachment to your existing life, focus instead on the projects that will create the life you want right now—instead of the life you plan to sell to someone else.

Some home values are directly related to the physical space. If you desire a home where you can raise a large family, you need enough bedrooms to accommodate that family comfortably. If a home is too small, it will need physical expansion.

What about emotional values like "restoration"? A house might fit a family comfortably, with enough bathrooms and a spacious kitchen, but you might feel there is no place where you can experience solitude and restore yourself. So get creative and consider what restoration, for you, requires. A restorative space could be:

- Backyard garden
- Cozy chair with a beverage table in a bedroom
- Tripped-out spa bathroom
- Gorgeous bath caddy with candle next to bathtub
- Under-the-stair reading nook
- Tiny meditation space in an unused closet

By identifying and focusing on your home values, you can prioritize home improvements that support the life you want to live. And if there are costs, you ensure you are spending money on what truly matters. By focusing on what you value, you can build your environment purposefully. When we are waffling over a new couch or a new rug, we are not deciding between objects. We are really making a choice about our need for togetherness (the couch) or our desire to feel more grounded (the rug).

What's Missing?

Often, when we feel that something in our life is lacking, we have simply forgotten to incorporate that idea into our space. We want joy, and when we look around our homes, we can feel that it's not there. We don't feel a sense of stability in our lives—and sure enough, there are signs of instability in the way we have set up our homes, such as objects that look like they are about to tip over. Simply by naming the values you want in your life, you will help inspire ideas for how to design and decorate your home so that it embodies those values.

FIND YOURSELF

What home values resonate most in the lists you made?

What changes (big or small) would you make to your home to embody more of your values?

4

THE STORY YOUR
HOME IS TELLING

As a teenager, I led tours through the second floor at Wheatland, the Federalist mansion of President James Buchanan, America's only bachelor president. My job was to guide visitors through the upstairs private quarters. There, I told the story of Buchanan's niece, Harriet, who served as his First Lady while in office, and I shared stories of the curiosities of home life in the mid-nineteenth century—such as sleeping on rope beds with straw mattresses.

The real drama happened downstairs. Sometimes I would tag along on the first-floor tours to brush up on my history or just to get a sense of the people on the tour before my turn. Two of the more passionate guides were regulars who couldn't have had more different approaches. One woman liked to wear a black mourning dress and spoke in a rich Brooklyn accent. She was only interested in the facts, what we know from the physical record, and she waved off many of the juicier parts of the Buchanan story—that he might have been gay, that a broken engagement might have caused his fiancée to take her own life. The other guide was a veteran actor who dressed like he had just stepped off Dickens's stage. He loved to keep things open-ended, and he told stories in a way that evoked the highs and lows of Buchanan's life.

The first guide spoke like an archaeologist. The second transported listeners to a different time.

Maybe you can guess which one I preferred, but that isn't really the point. Each guide commanded the room with their presence and took charge of everyone's experience. They decided what parts of the story were worth paying attention to, and by telling their version of the story, the walls came alive. Both guides evoked the spirits of the people who had lived there.

Home Is the Story We Choose to Live With

No one has more power in a room than the person telling the story. Your home is the best place to tell yours. Home is the place to surround yourself with *the story you choose to live with* about yourself. We each do this by our choice of furniture, by how we lay out a room, by the materials we use, by the ways we play with the unseen worlds of music, scent, and energy, by the visual cues that decorate the walls. Intentionally or not, we tell our story with the way we tend to our home, how we clutter and declutter, and how we identify (or don't) with what we surround ourselves with.

Nobody is their home, not exactly, even when they command it with a storyteller's sense of ownership, curiosity, and power. Our home is more like an active energy field that hugs and shapes us, like a cell membrane holds a cell nucleus. We exist in an energetic exchange with our home.

To a degree, this has always been true, but in past centuries, not everyone had the ability to shape their home as they wished, and those who did usually used their home to tell a story of wealth and privilege. Homes were status symbols that signified a person's place in society. In the twentieth century, the growth of the middle class changed society, and homes changed, too. Homeowners more often looked to their peers and to magazines and media to decide what story they wanted their homes to tell about them. But one thing didn't change: Home was a story told to the rest of the world.

Today, old ideas of social status are not only being questioned but actively turned on their heads. Various lifestyle movements are arising that embody the different ways people express their values. Social media, the trend of families choosing to live closer together, and the recent pandemic-related shift to remote jobs are also having impacts. You might say, our era is now a time when we use social media to tell our stories to the world, but we use our homes to tell our stories to ourselves.

Use Interior Design to Tell Your Story

Our homes are potent places to tell our stories. They allow us to edit and create our stories in physical space. Homes are not just shelters. In a literal sense, they become the stories we choose to live with. When we display an object from the past, such as a saved letter in a beautiful box, it reminds us of an important relationship or an important time. A family portrait can be a symbol of shared values and dreams. Even a favorite chair can signal our priorities and how we want to take up space in this world.

What stories is your home already telling? Some stories enliven homes particularly well. Consider this list of story types and see if you connect with any of them. Make a note of which ones and dream about how you might bring more of that story into your home.

Heritage: Your inherited shared culture, religion, background, or ethnic identity.

Interests and hobbies: The activities you feel passionate about.

Personality: Your unique, exuberant self.

Historical era: The period of history you feel made for.

Aesthetic: The artistic or design styles that you consider beautiful and which move your spirit.

Achievement: The great things you've accomplished.

Family: The people you consider family, both relatives and chosen family.

Mission: What you care about and what moves you to action.

Geography: The town, city, or region you identify with—even if it's not the place you currently live.

Travel: The places you've visited that make you come alive.

Rewrite Stories You Don't Want to Live With

Stories have power—so much power that when we get stuck in negative stories, we sometimes have to fight and claw our way out of them. Anyone who has ever been to therapy knows this. Negative stories can hold us back, disempower us, make us numb, even deceive us. At one time, certain stories may have been true or helped us make sense of a difficult experience, but when we recognize that those stories are holding us back, it's time to rewrite them. Consider for yourself: Are there old stories you tell yourself that aren't serving you anymore? And are there ways that your home is currently supporting these stories?

Now consider how you might redesign or redecorate your home to tell a different, more joyful, more empowering story—one that looks forward, not back. For example, if you have recently separated from a partner, it may be time to redo your bedroom or just refresh your bed sheets. Or if you're embarking on new training or education, you take a good look at your work space. As you consider this, have compassion for yourself. Life is challenging, and we meet those challenges as best we can. Remember, surviving is itself heroic, and our past does not have to define our future. How might you take a story, great or small, that no longer serves you and replace it with one that does?

When we know what stories and messages we are ready to discard and which we want to champion, we are in a better position to make choices for how to set up, decorate, and evolve with our homes. Ultimately, our goal is to create a space where we look around and think: *Yes, I love this story.*

FIND YOURSELF

What are some of the stories you'd like to give
space to in your home?

What are some of the stories about yourself that are no
longer helpful? How might you rewrite them in your home?

5

IF **THESE WALLS** COULD **TALK**

I have been in conversation with spaces forever, but it wasn't until I went through a major personal health crisis that I realized the power of "talking to my home." About half a decade ago, a perfect storm of physical injuries and health problems caused a nerve injury that made it impossible for me to sit without pain. For the first few months, all I did was lie down in front of the fireplace—a floor slug—and wait for the pain to go away (it didn't). I numbed myself by watching procedural dramas.

Then one day, after assuming my miserable position and resigning myself to being a TV-watching pile of goo, I suddenly felt the room begin to vibrate. I looked around and realized that, while my mind was overwhelmed with a running commentary of everything that was wrong with me, my situation, and the world, there was nothing wrong, per se, with the room. I felt held. Sunlight streamed through the window. I focused on how the floor supported my body. Then I noticed a thin layer of dust covering my shelves and furniture, and I felt the room call out to me.

Then I did what generations of grandmas have done whenever times get tough. I puttered. I got up, wet a cloth, and dusted my shelves. The act felt almost tender, full of affection. I felt the objects through the cloth as I dusted them. When Adam came home, he noticed that I had "cleaned up." But really, I had found a way to enjoy being in my body. Instead of wallowing, I had absorbed the good feeling of the room. I didn't feel better because my house was clean (though that didn't hurt). I felt better because I had stepped into a flow of caring for and tending to my space, and in turn myself. My home and I had had an emotional tête-à-tête and figured some things out, together.

In the aftermath, Adam and I reconfigured our life around my new disability. In addition to playing detective to solve my health mystery, I got a standing desk, we started eating dinner at the kitchen counter, we acquired a stargazer camping chair that allowed me to recline without activating my pain, and we created boundaries around social engagements like dinner parties. I hadn't wanted to make changes to accommodate what I was going through. I had resisted change, hoping my life and my body would just magically snap back to normal, and then after making some positive adjustments, I immediately wondered why I had waited so long feeling miserable. Today, I can give myself some grace for needing that time on the floor to gather my reserves of hope. Sometimes, we wallow. But I also now know I have the resilience to get up and not stay there. Now, instead of getting lost in conversations in my head, I talk to my house.

Care for Yourself by Caring for Your Space

When faced with problems, it's easy to get trapped inside our head. Negative chatter takes over—a running commentary on what isn't right, what has to be fixed, and who is causing the problems (even if it's ourselves). We fixate on whatever has done us wrong. In these moments, choosing to talk to our space instead of listening to a kaleidoscope of mental worry and rumination can be a powerful way to step outside of our thoughts and into the true peace and beauty of what is actually happening around us.

And if, in a moment of dark reflection, we look around and don't like what we see—our space is the opposite of beauty and peace—well, that's an invitation to make a change. This movement and activity helps negative emotions and energies become unstuck, so they move through and out of our bodies and flow somewhere else. Physically moving around our space—having a little chat session with our house—can calm the nerves and distract us from unpleasant feelings.

Then, by reinvigorating our space, we help reinvigorate ourselves. The goal isn't to overhaul our house, but simply to listen to whatever feels right intuitively in the moment. That might be dusting or a bit of redecorating. The point is to use our sense of our space to check in emotionally and transform stuck energy.

Start by expanding your awareness of a particular room in your home—or of the whole place, especially if it's an apartment. In whatever position feels comfortable, sit (ha!) or stand in the middle of the room, close your eyes, and notice the overall feeling. Take the room's temperature while taking a few calming breaths. Notice any scents. Listen to the ambient sounds—street noise, birdsong, the hum of your refrigerator. Simply observe without judgment for as long as you want and mentally and emotionally connect with the room itself. Become a single entity, as if you are the nucleus of a single cell. Expand your awareness of the room until you feel as if your entire self is taking up the entire space. Enjoy this sense of connection, as if you are part of the furniture, the lighting, the shelves, your home.

Then, if anything feels off, if something calls to you to make a mild readjustment, take action. Make that change.

Our Homes Should Change as We Change

Life is constantly changing and so are we, and our homes need to change with us so they reflect who we are right now, not who we were yesterday. Sometimes we resist change, as I did with my injury. We don't like it, and we try to avoid or deny it.

Change can be a gut punch sometimes. I'll never forget when I rewatched *Beetlejuice* with my kids and realized that I no longer identified with Lydia, the dark teenaged daughter who can see ghosts, but with the sculptor stepmom Delia Deetz—who says she will go crazy unless she can remake every room in the house. *Why is she the villain in this movie?* I thought.

Regularly "talking with your home" is one way to recognize when you might be stuck or trapped in a particular stage of life. These conversations can help you see how you are changing—your needs, your desires, your aesthetic urges, your passions, your primal responses. People who work in interior design believe that walls really *do* talk. They tell a story about the occupants. And if the story in your home doesn't align with the person you are or aspire to be, you can change your space so it does align.

Homes are not established, finished dioramas. I consider them constantly evolving, immersive works of art that change as the inhabitants change. Perhaps it is a bold, unprovable claim to say that there is a spatial solution for every problem (get on that, neuroscience!), but my experience with my own home and in my work with clients has convinced me that working with spaces allows for both subtle and profound shifts in outlook that help us process the changes in our lives. By consciously changing our home to reflect our changing circumstances and sense of self, we are far less likely to feel emotionally blocked or stuck in a metaphorical swamp.

In simplest terms, working on your home is a means of working on yourself. How you decorate your home is how you communicate with your energetic field and with yourself. So treat your space as a blank canvas to explore and express your evolving identity, sense of purpose, and aspirations.

Recognize When Change Is Needed

Some people like novelty and some people like consistency. Some people are perfectly happy living in a home where everything stays the same all the time, while others need the fresh perspective of moving around furniture, changing wall colors, reshaping rooms, and hanging new art. One personality type is not better than another, and my intention isn't to suggest that change, in itself, is necessary or even best.

However, by having regular "talks" with your home, you can recognize when you feel stuck, and by making changes in your space, you can help yourself get unstuck. Someone who likes novelty, who is constantly redoing rooms, might need stability and grounding in their home to balance this tendency. A person who loves consistency might start to chafe if they have lived with the same furniture for their entire lives and their home feels like a museum to their past. We often move through life unconsciously and get trapped in assumptions about who we are. The key is to recognize when this happens and to look for solutions in the home that free us from whatever is confining or holding us back.

More Than Spring Cleaning: Regularly Reassess Your Space

I suggest regularly reassessing your space as a self-reflective tool. Magazines will tell you that spring is the time to purge the home, to banish dust bunnies and freshen up, but listen to yourself. Become attuned to your own rhythms.

For me, as soon as the sun starts returning by the end of January, my Purge Beast reappears. In summer, the first couple of times I got a burning urge to sew cloth napkins, I just went with it and praised my own creative spirit. After a couple years of that, I realized I always need to feel the hum of fabric under my sewing machine in July. When the air turns crisp in fall, I become a wild woman with clippers scouting out dried pampas grass growing near our local train tracks. In winter, I tone down all of the brighter colors in my home like clockwork. Pay attention to your creative urges at home, and honor your own timelines.

If you're unsure what your personal rhythms are, use social media. Make a practice of documenting any puttering you do at home (privately is fine), and soon you will start to recognize patterns. That was how I discovered that my own rhythms at home are 100 percent predictable. In fact, my urges to clean and redo are in complete harmony with the seasons of the Pacific Northwest, where I live.

Beyond the sheer joy of being in conversation with your home throughout the seasons, the most important time to reassess your space is when you feel stuck or when life is moving too fast and feels out of control. When you're bored, or don't like a life situation, making larger-scale changes within the home can shake up your energy. Perhaps changing something powerful—like a wall color—will agitate the energy in your life. By that same token, when life feels chaotic or is moving too fast, maybe focus on adding more to your home life—more coziness, more objects, more calming hues, more textured upholstery. Anything that dials down your nervous system and makes you feel less in your head and more in your body can give you a greater sense of control and peace.

Like What You Like

Is there a magic moment when someone realizes the allure of, say, blue hydrangeas—or anything they didn't notice before as special? As you move through life, your taste will change. New things will resonate with you. Honor those impulses. Get in the habit of acquiring and displaying what you find attractive, and leave behind what doesn't inspire you anymore, even if it once did. Do this without shame or deference to anybody else's taste. Tastemakers will always be opining about what is in or out, what works or doesn't work. But make your home the place where you show up more truthfully than anywhere else, where you accept who you are now while exploring who you are becoming.

One of my favorite style trends of these past few years has been the rise of the grandmillennial décor style, where elements such as floral couches and ruffled trims have gone from stodgy and passé to fresh and fun. A new generation of homemakers and designers is doing what feels good to them—which is to incorporate design elements that their grandmothers might have been drawn to. Nostalgic moments have found a new life as people reach for comfort and story in an unapologetic way. After writers gave this cultural moment a name, it freed everyone up to be inspired by a playful mix of the stodgy and the modern. Trends happen when people listen to themselves and respond to what they like without caring what others think.

WHAT'S YOUR VIBE?

Most interiors aren't just one style or another. Homes mix elements to express the particular vibe of the humans inside. To help you discover your vibe, I've provided a list of opposing concepts below. For each, consider and mark where you fall on the scale, then use this to evaluate your space. How well do you fulfill these attributes? Let what you find guide your choices when making changes.

Simple	Complex
Loud	Quiet
Lush	Flat
Sensual	Intellectual
Colorful	Neutral
Furry	Smooth
Shiny	Matte
Patterned	Solid
Grand	Cozy
Personal	Anonymous
Formal	Informal
Activating	Calming
Historical	Modern
Fresh	Time-worn
Bright	Moody
Fun	Serious

We live in a time of great choice, with market access to basically everything under the sun. What would your home look like if you allowed yourself to resonate with what you found attractive and inspiring, regardless of whether it matched the latest trends or fit what other people expected? What if you embraced your "guilty pleasures" and accepted them as an expression of your deepest self? What if you made your home the place you explored the person you are becoming?

That said, do you know what your personal vibe or aesthetic is? Many people don't. However, if you can pinpoint how you want to feel in your space—the "vibe" that embodies you—then you'll be able to choose the stylistic elements that naturally express it. A trend is

social. It identifies what is happening in the world, outside your home. A vibe is personal; it speaks to what's going on inside you. There's nothing wrong with paying attention to the design world (I certainly do) to help discover what you like. But translate and incorporate trends so they reflect what you love and are authentic to your own life. Vibes are full-body experiences. That's what home should be.

Move Twenty-Seven Things

If you feel stuck and don't know what to do to change your space, try simply moving some things around. By switching things up, you engage in an energetic conversation with your house. This isn't "redecorating," per se. There is no plan, no place anything "should" go. You are experimenting and exploring to see if a new arrangement might be beneficial. Even if you don't know what will help, trying something different often feels good in the moment.

One easy maxim for instigating life change is to physically move twenty-seven things. In feng shui, twenty-seven is a magical number for disrupting recycled energy patterns. By moving twenty-seven things that haven't been moved in a year, you effectively activate the energy moving through your home. I love this idea, since it doesn't require buying anything. You can work with what you have and still come away with a new perspective on your life and whatever problems you are facing. For instance, by doing something as simple as moving a favorite sitting chair to the opposite side of the room, you can't help but look at things differently; you have literally changed your view.

The twenty-seven things don't have to be big. Rearrange favorite objects on a shelf, switch existing art to new walls, place floor lamps and blanket baskets differently. You may be surprised at what happens with just a modest reconfiguring of your environment.

FIND YOURSELF

Identify one way you have already been talking to your house.

Write a paragraph about the current overall vibe in your home and your feelings about it. Then write a paragraph about how you would like it to feel.

SPACE

PREPARE YOUR ENVIRONMENT FOR YOUR STORY

6

MEET your COLLABORATOR

'll never forget the first time I had a conversation with my new neighbor after we moved into our current home. Without a beat, he asked me if I knew that the father of the household who had lived there had to move because he had lost his job (I hadn't, and was taken aback by his forthcomingness about people's tragedies). What might have seemed like a rude question was actually quite relevant. He was concerned. I found the information helpful in the years thereafter, when I began researching and understanding house energies and how they tend to stick around, even as inhabitants change. About half a year later, I discovered a pipe leak near my front door that had existed since construction. I had bought what is known in feng shui as a crying house—a home where hidden leaks or problems with plumbing in general seem to coincide with households experiencing misfortune.

When we look at homes, we tend to focus on what we can easily quantify, like square footage, number of bedrooms and bathrooms, the price, and the likelihood of appreciation for our investment. Yet I believe that the spirit of a house, the specific thoughtfulness behind its spatial layout, the makeup of its materials, and the way it accommodates what we value in our lives is just as important. In addition, knowing its history will help clarify how its past and the energies of its previous inhabitants could potentially affect us.

Spaces tend to accumulate the vibes of the people who inhabit them. Even when custom homes are built on land that looks like a blank slate, every space has what is called "predecessor energy."

For instance, here's a story that really blew my mind: A friend of mine bought a first home with her husband that was sold to them by a couple that had recently separated. Over time, my friend's relationship also ended, while the other couple got back together in a new home. Just watching the whole thing unfold made me curious about the impact of houses and prior energies. Was my friend's new house predisposed to make living in partnership difficult?

This chapter focuses on developing a more active energetic relationship with your home. By getting to know your home's existing energy—by gathering its history and touring your own home with fresh eyes—you can assess how energy is moving in and out of your life. Then, by using space clearing to imbue the house with your own energy (see chapter 8), you can ensure that you create a more harmonious and beneficial relationship with your space.

Discover Your Home's History

Finding out the history of a home can be challenging. Real estate agents don't like to reveal any potentially negative details about a home that may prevent or skew a sale. As the US housing stock ages, it becomes even harder to gather a full accounting of the major life events that transpired in a home. Nevertheless, any information is good information and can aid you as you create your own energy imprint.

Talking to neighbors can be the most beneficial approach to finding out a space's history. When people care about their neighborhood, they pay attention to who comes and goes, and some will eagerly give you all the gossip about whoever used to live in your home. In my neighborhood, I'm afraid that person might be me! One friend, who lives two doors down, calls me "the mayor." Befriend your street's mayor and get ready—they will have a lot to share! Frankly, I am always shocked when people move onto our block and *don't* ask about who lived in their house before.

As you conduct your reconnaissance, be sure to ask about past structural or mechanical issues, major cataclysmic events like flooding and fires, and whether the owners maintained the home well. Also ask about the people—what they were like and if any unusual events were known to have transpired behind the walls.

Then keep a log of this history—anything you learn about the home and its previous occupants. Past tragedies, whether or not animals lived there, whether children brought energy to the home—small details can have a big impact on how later inhabitants' lives unfold there and can often indicate where energy needs to be shifted.

MEET YOUR SPACE AS IF
FOR THE FIRST TIME

Think back to the first time you encountered your home space—how it brimmed with possibilities and hope. Channel that feeling as you do this exercise. Create some distance between yourself and your home in order to experience it as it is, outside of your daily routine.

Mark out a good hour (depending on your home's size) to do a home tour of your own house. Do this with a notebook in hand, so you can write down your impressions as you go. Choose a time of day when you feel high energy and open to possibilities but not particularly self-critical. It's important to be in a calm, relaxed, and positive frame of mind and not hurried, busy, or preoccupied. You want to be open to your feelings and intuition as you evaluate the subtle differences in the vibrations of your home.

Begin by standing outside in front of your house so you can see your home in its entirety. Take a few breaths to center yourself and let your eyes blur just a bit: Take in the essence of your home. In your notebook, write down some big-picture feelings about what you feel while standing outside.

Enter your home through the front door. Announce yourself to your home and express gratitude for it. Out loud or in your mind, let it know that you appreciate that it is taking care of you, that you are going to be spending some time getting to know it better, and that you are there to help.

Then, as much as possible, move clockwise through each of your home's rooms. Clockwise is preferred because, in feng shui, energy (or chi) is said to swirl in that direction. In each space, pay attention to how you respond, and write down notes whenever any of the following happen:

- You feel encouraged to speed up or to stop and linger.
- You are bothered by what you see, especially clutter.
- You have a strong emotional response—joy, nostalgia, anger, whatever.
- You sense that the energy feels particularly alive or dead.
- You notice any visible physical impediments or concerns.

Do the same, moving clockwise, for any additional floors your home may have.

As you go through your house, try not to judge yourself, either for your reactions or for what you encounter. Just make a note of that pile of paperwork that's been gnawing at you for weeks; we'll fix that in chapter 7. Just be curious about what you find, as if you are an anthropologist learning about someone from a different time or society. Pay attention to where the design of your home is naturally encouraging you to move and to which areas feel less inviting. When you are finished, thank your home for what it has shown you.

FIND YOURSELF

What do you know about the history of your home
and its previous occupants?

During your home tour, did you notice any patterns about where
your home tends to accumulate dead spaces or vibrant energy?

7

CONSIDER the VIBRANCY
of YOUR OBJECTS

brake for estate sales. One spring day, Adam and I saw an ad for a funeral parlor that was going out of business (who knew they did that?). They were offloading nearly a century's worth of stuff, and we raced to join a throng of scavengers in the cavernous, midcentury building. There were many fascinating objects—giant hanging tapestries, old letterpress blocks, and light fixtures that were, as the saying goes, to die for.

In a back room, I spotted two matching orange Victorian chairs. One was in a sad state of decrepitude. But the other was relatively fine, with unblemished upholstery and just a few scuffs on the wood. I thought it was the prettiest in the room, and I snatched it for twenty dollars. Score! My husband, who tends to rehabilitate everything he comes across, glowed.

Like Houses, Objects Hold Energy

Have you ever dropped something and apologized to it? I do this all the time without even thinking. People often anthropomorphize objects, imbuing them with spirit, personality, and meaning. Children do this naturally, creating entire make-believe stories for objects. But as adults, we usually grow out of this, and many people don't take seriously the idea that objects could be "alive" in any way. We are encouraged to care for objects only if they are useful or beautiful. This egocentric thinking is part of what's led to our current throwaway culture.

I believe strongly in the spirit of things. When we live with objects—be they a chair or a frying pan, a bed duvet or a vase—we create a subtle energetic conversation with them. Further, how we choose to acquire, live with, and discard objects is a subject of great moral inquiry, especially in regards to the environment and climate change.

The art world is certainly at the forefront of exploring this exchange. My artist friend Annika once repurposed an entire couch, making it into usable containers, like a backpack, boxes, and a cabinet. The rub? Whoever purchased the art pieces had to sign an agreement assuming responsibility for the materiality of the object, meaning they couldn't throw it out or pass it on without first contacting her. I often think about this project—what a better state the world would be in if we honored materials this thoughtfully.

Another concern is more personal. Social scientists have found that we can only maintain about 150 meaningful, stable social relationships. If we include our relationships with objects, we are truly overloaded in this era of overabundance. Or consider a room packed with an overaccumulation of objects: How can we have that many conversations going on at once and maintain any grace or control?

As you consider the vibrancy of your spaces, also pay attention to the objects they contain. Do they just take up space, do they drag you down, or do they awaken an inner aliveness and add to the vital energy in your home?

If Objects Could Talk

All objects—from the smallest ceramic tchotchke to the largest piece of furniture—carry stories with them based on how they are made, what they are composed of, what contexts they have existed in, who has used them and why, how far they have traveled, and the reasons they are acquired. Like learning the history of our home, it's helpful to know as much about the objects we buy as possible. Since it's hard to discover the provenance of stuff, this isn't something to obsess over. But as much as possible, pay close attention to an object's vibrancy before bringing it into your home.

Of course, even this level of consideration isn't always possible. Our time, incomes, and circumstances are limited, and sometimes we have to buy whatever we need that fits our budget. In some ways, it is a mark of privilege to be able to even think about an object's provenance. On the other hand, in my mind, it is a revolutionary act to build a home slowly, consciously, and with the ethics of material ownership in mind. So I believe, when we have a choice, we should consider our objects before we buy them. But even more than that, once objects are in our home, we should become conscious of their energetic impact.

The funeral chair turned out to be a lesson in how some objects are only beautiful within a certain context, as well as in what our attraction to objects can teach us about ourselves. As soon as Adam and I got our funeral chair in the car, we noticed the flat, deadening stink of cigarette smoke. Then, when we placed it in our living room, we finally saw it for what it was: a place where, for half a century, friends and family members had grieved the passing of their loved ones. Even the orange wool upholstery, which had seemed so bright amid all the junk, looked suddenly drab and sad. We experienced a familiar form of buyer's remorse—when something that was stunning in the store suddenly loses its sparkle at home.

Our action was swift. To deal with the smell, we placed the chair in the sun, scrubbed it several times with a gentle dish soap, emptied an entire bottle of Febreeze on it, and left the chair outside for the entire summer. Then, I performed an energy clearing on the chair (similar to what I describe in chapter 8). Eventually, we brought it back inside. While the chair itself seemed less sad, it still seemed off, and so did I. What had drawn me to a chair that had absorbed so much death?

Then it hit me. When we visited the funeral home sale, I was in the process of investigating my deepest childhood wound—my father's abandonment of our family. Online, I was meeting with my father weekly to work through three decades' worth of difficult feelings. Had I been drawn to the funeral chair because I was feeling so much grief and wanted to make room for it in my home? Further, was buying the chair a way to hold on to my grief, which I couldn't imagine letting go of? I'm convinced both were true.

An Object's Energy Can Change

Did I get rid of the chair? No, I worked through my feelings, and years later, the chair found a place in our bedroom. Today, I usually walk by it without even thinking about it. It's just become part of the scene.

Meaning is fluid. Our attachments to objects can and will change over time. Further, two people can have vastly different responses to the same object. Adam did not respond to the chair the way I did, and together, we discovered it fit in our home.

A good example are objects from childhood, like a stuffed animal. A child might need a beloved bear to feel safe at night, then bury it in a closet as a teen, and then treasure it as an adult because it's imbued with childhood memories. It's helpful to become aware of how objects impact us, but those impacts can change as we change. During a stressful period, we might be drawn to objects that speak to those emotions, and once those emotions pass, the object might lose its power, too. Indeed, by recognizing our energetic relationship with objects, we can sometimes identify stuck places and old stories that need rewriting.

Today, when I purchase something for our home, I imagine I am buying a gift for our space. In the same way I'd carefully consider the right gift for a special person, I apply that same consideration to my relationship with my home. I am also careful not to do too much purchasing when I am in a foul mood. Indulging in retail therapy—or buying something to feel better—never transforms my feelings. It simply results in a souvenir of a state I don't want replicated in my space.

Ideally, everything in your home should align with the story of who you are becoming. Because of their usefulness, their energy, and your attachment to them, objects should feel vibrant and alive. But when objects are no longer useful and don't feel energetically supportive, consider getting rid of them. This is what the decluttering process is all about. However, if you are unsure, take your time making a decision. You can always move certain objects into "limbo" until your feelings change or clarify and you know whether you are ready to let them go.

The Special Case of Inherited Objects

I recently helped clear out my childhood home and discovered that my mother had been storing my family's old spinning wheel. My uncle had inherited it, but he had left it behind when he moved to Brazil. I pulled this artifact out from behind boxes and placed it in the middle of the living room, prepared to make the case for getting rid of it.

With a little investigating, I learned a few things. For one, this spinning wheel was not some long-lost tool pumped by the feet of my beloved ancestors. My grandparents, who like antiques, had purchased it at an auction and then allowed no one to ever touch it. For everyone in the family (except me), it was a storehouse of fond memories, almost a kind of familial wayfinding device.

That weekend, my uncle arrived, loaded the spinning wheel into his car, and took it to a storage facility. When I posted photos of this on social media, my family erupted in a chorus of hurrahs and likes. Everyone wanted to keep the wheel—even if no one wanted to live with it.

Inherited objects deserve particular consideration, since these relics become attached to the people we miss and the places that formed us. Family antiques add a gravitas and beauty to a home and embody the larger story of ourselves. Any antique might do this, even if it isn't a family heirloom, if we feel connected to what it represents. Objects from the past can give homes an air of timelessness, and family objects can provide a sense of connectedness and continuity.

But a house filled with antiques can also start to feel like a museum—*don't touch the spinning wheel!* You don't have to keep objects just because they were meaningful to a relative who passed them along to you. So if you choose to keep an inherited object, make sure it is truly meaningful *to you*, and then give it a place of honor in your home so it adds to your story.

The Allure of Hopeful Objects

Sometimes we hold on to items because they represent something we want to change. I call these "hopeful objects." Our hope is that, by virtue of possessing them, we will one day fulfill what they promise.

One of my clients, Georgia, had one of those quilt display racks in the corner of her bedroom. Georgia's quilt was unfinished. She had started making it twenty years before as a gift for her brother's marriage. Since then, her relationship with her brother had become complicated. They were barely in touch, but Georgia held out hope that something would change between them, and the display rack represented that hope.

I counseled Georgia either to finish the quilt and give it to her brother or to remove it from her bedroom. Georgia decided that she was trapped in a stage of grief about her brother, and she wanted to move toward acceptance. So she donated the unfinished quilt to a group that repurposes quilt supplies for refugees, and she let go of thinking her relationship with her brother might change.

Hope can be a beautiful thing, but it can also lodge itself in our objects instead of staying perched in our soul. Hopeful objects can be old clothes that don't fit anymore, craft supplies from projects we haven't finished (and maybe never will), and books we will never read. They are anything whose usefulness we've moved beyond. If you identify a hopeful object, ask what action you can take to bring this hope to fruition. If nothing can—say, a physical injury prevents you from playing tennis—then let go of that hope and give away that tennis racket. By taking action to make your hope real, you will discover whether the object truly deserves a place in your home.

PRACTICE EVALUATING OBJECTS

Decluttering is all about making room for change and new energies while also simplifying and making life less stressful. However, it doesn't have to be approached as a multiday, whole-house cleanse. You can declutter one room at a time, one closet at a time, or even one object at a time. In essence, whenever you notice an object that isn't useful and doesn't serve you, consider removing it.

To get used to this process of evaluation, practice assessing all the objects in a single room, but without feeling any obligation to get rid of anything. Simply consider and classify all the objects into one of the four categories below. One thing you will notice is whether you tend to accumulate one category more than others. Some people are natural historians, while others have difficulty parting with anything that might have a future use.

Ask yourself the following questions, and any object that doesn't fit any category is, of course, a potential candidate for removal.

Useful: Do you need it, now or in the foreseeable future?

Beautiful: Do you find it beautiful in this moment?

Inherited: Does it represent who you are, your family and culture, or your past?

Hopeful: Does it represent something you hope to achieve, accomplish, or change?

FIND YOURSELF

What objects in your home represent parts of your past you embrace and want to live with, and what part of your story do they embody?

Are there objects in your home that represent parts of your past you want to let go of, and might getting rid of these objects help to symbolically let them go?

8

PERFORM A RITUAL
TO CLEAR YOUR SPACE

ituals are meaning we make through action. They are simple, repeated behaviors that can happen in any setting. They involve words, prescribed acts, and often objects imbued with meaning, and they are performed in a predictable sequence that can be repeated. Rituals have been part of religious practices in communities across the globe and throughout history, but they certainly don't have to be spiritual. They don't reflect superstition.

While we can create our own personalized rituals, they aren't made up out of thin air. Ritual actions may be quiet, but they carry high stakes for how we move through the world with dignity, consciousness, and generosity. They are nothing less than how we practice what is important to us while building the relationships, communities, and states of being that make life worth living.

At home, rituals can be as simple as lighting a candle before guests arrive or making the bed in the morning. The repeated behavior is a way to focus on and embody our intention: to welcome people into our home, to prepare ourselves for the day. Rituals humanize life, reflect our priorities, and add structure to activities.

I highly recommend establishing personalized rituals that focus on receiving desired outcomes. Rituals have been proven to increase self-confidence, to improve our performance on tasks, and to reduce overall anxiety.[4] They can help us move through grief or metabolize losses. They can put us in the right headspace for dealing with unexpected outcomes. They can lessen our worry about things that are out of our control and can ground us emotionally. It doesn't matter what the rituals look like so long as we imbue our words and actions with significance. Whether we say a few words of thanks before a meal or shake out our doormat weekly, rituals great and small make life better.

Here are some simple house rituals my clients have adopted with specific purposes in mind:

- Lighting a candle before dinner to create focus
- Shaking out the front mat each season to start fresh
- Wiping down the front door to welcome good energy
- Burning botanicals after cleaning to set intentions
- Making the bed daily to battle depression
- Fluffing pillows for an easy pick-me-up

How do you know if a ritual is right for you? First you have to try it out and see if it feels right. Most house rituals are deeply personal. They work as long as you are conscious about your intentions behind the ritual and it allows you to sink into the moment as you do it.

A HOME SPACE-CLEARING RITUAL

New rituals may feel awkward at first, but when practiced over time, they work a subtle magic on us. This home space-clearing ritual is one of the most helpful rituals for clearing stale or negative energy. Adapt this how you want to suit you and your space.

1. CHOOSE A HIGH-ENERGY DAY

Space clearing works when our energy is at its best. Plan to do this ritual when you are well rested emotionally and physically. If you are a person who menstruates, days seven to fourteen of your cycle are ideal.

2. TAKE A RITUAL BATH

Ritual bathing is part of many sacred practices, and I recommend taking a saltwater bath before doing this space clearing. The key to any ritual is not how simple or complex it is, but your intention behind it. While a bath isn't required, it's another ritual of spiritual renewal that helps shed the layers of modern life and return us to the vitality and sagacity of our mortal self.

What I recommend is soaking in a warm salt bath for about 30 minutes; three full cups of salt should be enough. Salt has a long history of ritual use in cleansing ceremonies. Energy practitioners believe it to be a perfect material for preparing your body, since saltwater conducts electricity better than regular water. Saltwater baths also stimulate circulation and reduce joint inflammation. Don't use table salt; choose 100 percent natural, authentic, harvested salts like Dead Sea salt, Himalayan salt, or sel gris. Epsom salt, which contains magnesium and is not actually a salt, is also a great muscle relaxant and works well.

3. ANOINT YOURSELF

Many cultures prescribe a self-massage following a ritual bath to restore the skin and the spirit, and I suggest doing the same. I like using

a pure carrier oil like jojoba oil or almond oil with a few drops of a favorite essential oil. Frankincense, lavender, rosemary, cedarwood, and chamomile are all excellent choices. Be sure to check your skin's reactivity to your blend before you perform massage. Also, you can dip your finger in your oil blend and touch your forehead while saying a mantra or phrase that has meaning for you.

4. CHOOSE YOUR GARMENTS

Does clothing matter? Not necessarily. But there is a performance aspect to space clearing, and personally, I love a good floor-length dress and bare feet as I move around my house and push out old energy. In essence, anything from your wardrobe that allows you to move freely will work, but avoid wearing jewelry, as anything metal can distract energy when working with spaces.

5. STATE YOUR INTENTION

When you're ready, stand in your space and announce out loud exactly what you will be doing and what you want to accomplish. State your intentions clearly.

This statement can be short and practical or elaborate and detailed. Whatever feels most appropriate and comfortable for you is what will serve you best. Experiment and see what happens. I personally like to make rituals as dramatic as possible, with all the bells and whistles. I was always too shy to go on stages, but I can be a priestess of magic and mystery when I'm on the set of my own making and no one is watching.

Here are some possible phrases:

> "I am clearing out old energies in order to make way for new movement in my life."

> "As I clear this space, I am making room for peace, prosperity, and happiness for all of this home's inhabitants."

> "By attending to this space, I am attracting new, vibrant energy into my home."

6. MAKE SOME NOISE

Use sounds and vibration to break up the dead energy in your rooms. One approach is to clap your hands, or use a hand bell, a drum, or any other noisemaker. Move around the periphery of each room, and go from floor to ceiling, while ringing a bell or clapping your hands to shake up the energies.

7. SMUDGE EACH ROOM

Make sure to open the windows, hold a plate under the materials so embers don't drop on the floor or furniture, and wave the material to ensure the smoke gets into the corners.

8. BLESS YOUR HOUSE

When you've finished clearing every room, express a blessing for your house. This doesn't need to be complicated. Merely speak from your heart. Give voice to the life you desire in your home. I often recommend that people write out this blessing beforehand and read it out loud. If you wish, include the blessings of any other people in the house. Talk to them about what they want and include their desires.

Here are some prompts to get you started:

When I think about what I want for us at home, I envision . . .

May this house bless me with . . .

May our lives at home be filled with . . .

Let me know every day that . . .

Keep us safe from . . .

Empower me to . . .

If you have written your house blessing, consider displaying it, either privately or prominently. I love the look of an easily removable acrylic wall frame that can be changed out easily. Or, to keep this blessing private, hide it somewhere in the middle of the home, such as tucked under a lamp, behind a framed photograph, or under a throw rug.

Burning botanicals, or smudging, is a way to move a spiritual intention into physical space. This ancient ritual has appeared in every culture. It connects us with the element of fire, which is passionate and powerful, both physically and spiritually. By lighting the material, we reclaim our power, and we can see and smell that power diffuse into our space as it burns. However, remember to open the windows, since any smoke can be toxic in large quantities.

Palo santo: The resinous wood palo santo ("holy wood") remains a material of choice for space clearing because of its rich, sweet, campfire-like, slightly lemony scent, its versatility, and its centuries of ritual use in South and Central America, where it grows. Buy from a reputable company with an ethical approach to harvesting, since deforestation is an issue in some places.

Sage: Sage is often used in smudging ceremonies and for traditional medicinal use around the world, since it contains polyphenol compounds beneficial to cognition (reducing oxidative stress, improving memory function, and increasing focus and attention).[5] While no research has been done on the medical benefits of burning sage, metaphysical practitioners designate specific uses for different types of sage, including a few below.

- **White sage:** Also known as California or bee sage. If you use white sage to clear negative energies, prepare to receive teachings.

- **Spanish lavender sage:** This type of sage helps bring you into the present moment and enhance memory.

- **Blue sage:** Also known as grandmother sage, this botanical purifies, draws on spiritual strength, and removes malevolent spirits.

- **Black sage:** Also known as mugwort, this encourages visions and heals at the soul level.

Sweetgrass: This resilient grass grows across climates near bodies of water in North America and Eurasia. Native Americans have a history of ceremonial use. With a sweet scent like its name, it is braided and dried, making it a beautiful tool to hold in the hand during a home ritual. Burn it especially to purify thoughts and evoke healing and peace.

Permanent House Blessings

A space-clearing ceremony includes a house blessing that reflects the hopes of the moment, but you can create a more permanent, ongoing blessing in your home. Simply write or choose a blessing and put it on display.

Write your own house blessing or borrow the words of someone else. Use a quote from a spiritual text or lyrics from a favorite song. Memorialize a family member's favorite saying. A permanent house blessing doesn't have to look or sound like anyone else's. In fact, it shouldn't. Feel free to use whatever phrasing encapsulates your greatest hopes for your life at home.

If you wish, frame the blessing, or as a craft project, embody it in some other material. Display your house blessing prominently, so everyone who lives there and comes through the door will encounter it.

Make a House Ritual Drawer

Finally, another possibility is to convert a classic junk drawer into a space that holds everything you use for space-clearing rituals, such as candles, burn sticks, clearing bells, incense, and a gorgeous journal (or maybe even this book!). Ideally, this should be centrally located in your home.

Clear out a drawer, paint the inside a meaningful color, and cover the bottom of the drawer with wallpaper or a liner. Decorate it with your personal symbology, and even store your intentions here.

FIND YOURSELF

After doing the home space-clearing ritual, what shifts
did you notice in your home's energy?

What is one new ritual you'd like to incorporate
into your home life?

BUILD

DISCOVER DESIGN TOOLS TO CUE YOUR BEHAVIOR

9

CREATE A COLOR STORY

Through the years, I've probably made every design mistake with paint under the sun. That's okay. Homes are forgiving. And we can always repaint. No matter what experts tell us about color theory and how colors influence emotions and behavior, everyone has their own personal relationship with color. We attach memories to color. We play favorites with some parts of the spectrum and hate on others.

Color preferences also change throughout life. The colors we like today we may abhor tomorrow. We go through phases where we buy the same color clothing over and over without realizing it. We fall head over heels for trendy colors, and in short order, we're over it.

Color is a constant teacher, an infinite muse, a shifting symbolic landscape unto itself. Color responses are of course cultural. The colors signifying gender in one culture can mean something else entirely in a different culture. Our reactions are also evolutionary, meaning that human physiology responds to certain colors from the natural environment in predictable ways.

But above all, color is play. As this chapter explores how colors can make our lives at home more meaningful, I hope it inspires you to have fun.

A PSYCHOLOGICAL COLOR CHART

Let's look at what environmental psychologists and designers say about the effects of specific colors.

RED

Attributes: Stimulating, attention-grabbing, stops you in your tracks, signals anger and danger, encourages appetite

Impacts: We eat more in a red room or when using a red plate. We're more likely to become agitated.[6] Red is also distracting, making it a poor choice for work spaces.[7] In homes, a red accent wall was once common (hello, 1990s!), but designers use red sparingly, since it can overwhelm.

Try it out: Line a throw pillow with red; add a tomato-hued accent chair or a kilim rug.

BLUE

Attributes: Protective, calming, peaceful, honest, universally loved, secure, predictable

Impacts: Blue is the most preferred color for interiors, especially bedrooms, since it's calming. That said, it's less ideal in high-activity spaces.[8] The entire range of blues are favorites for designers. It's a classic.

Try it out: Blue-and-white stripes work great anywhere, or choose deep blue velvet for an upholstered piece.

PURPLE

Attributes: Inspiring, enlightening, can signify spirituality, magic, wealth, religion, wisdom, creativity, compassion

Impacts: Long associated with royalty and mysticism, purple regulates the brain and suppresses hunger. Designers tend to use it for moody, dark interiors, or to create fresh feelings with a light, lilac accent. It's a highly personalized color.

Try it out: Lilac on the walls can work as a neutral, a vase of purple blooms makes a magical arrangement, or one perfect accent chair can lend an air of mystery.

PINK

Attributes: Projects likability, romance, intuition, calmness, nurturing, groundedness, playfulness, love

Impacts: Some famous design experiments have shown how pink rooms cause prison inmates to become less agitated, but moderate pinks tend to be calming.[9] Further, pink rooms no longer signal palaces of femininity. Pink can look great in any space and take a lead role in earthy, calming interiors.

Try it out: A light mauve sofa feels pretty and Parisian, a muted rosy pink door pairs well with a black-and-white home, and bubblegum pink

adds a Palm Beach vibe to outdoor spaces.

ORANGE

Attributes: Encouraging, uplifting, fresh, stimulating, chatty, spontaneous, warm, youthful

Impacts: Orange feels warm and inspires excitement, vitality, and stimulation. It draws attention. Designers love playing with oranges, pairing it with blue (its complement on the color spectrum), and using it as an accent.

Try it out: Tangerine chairs work well for modern spaces, apricot can make a bright and energizing backdrop for living rooms, or pair with a dark blue for a sophisticated look.

GREEN

Attributes: Relaxing, balancing, signals harmony, health, vibrancy, prosperity, nature, growth

Impacts: Pale green is the most relaxing color on the spectrum, and all greens tend to reduce blood pressure. Walking in the woods provokes the same response.[10] It's an incredibly versatile color for interiors, whether as an accent color, a neutral, or a main color in restorative spaces.

Try it out: Green kitchen cabinets are an enduring trend. Try any incarnation, from deep forest to light sage. An olive green sofa fits a neutral palette, while a green abstract rug gives a moss-under-your-feet vibe.

YELLOW

Attributes: Happiness, optimism, positivity, creativity, earthiness, clarity, inspiration, uplift

Impacts: Yellow stimulates the heart and breathing while encouraging concentration and alertness. It's a great, warm color to bring into shared spaces, since it inspires joy and warmth.[11]

Try it out: Look for mustards and ochre accents, source a wallpaper with a pop of yellow, or get one perfect yellow-enameled pot to live permanently on your stovetop.

BLACK

Attributes: Conveys sophistication, protection, formality, strength, power, elegance, sadness

Impacts: Black can feel dangerous but also sophisticated and powerful. Across cultures, it is associated with depression and mourning. Designers usually use it sparingly as an accent. But recently, all-black kitchens and all-black buildings have made black seem like the new black.

Try it out: Use black hardware, paint your stair rail in a soft black, buy a black canopy bed, or paint your lower bath cabinets to look like the midnight sky.

GRAY

Attributes: Stabilizing, calming, intellectual, soothing, conservative, controlling, compromising

Impacts: People who live in gray industrialized areas demonstrate worse health than those who live in greener areas.[12] In the home, gray is a favorite neutral, but it needs other colors to come alive.

Try it out: Warm your walls with greige (beige + gray), ground a space with a gray geometric rug, balance a room with two symmetric accent chairs, or use gray throw cushions behind exciting accent pillows.

BROWN

Attributes: Stabilizing, simplifying, grounding, comforting, honest, reliable, predictable

Impacts: Brown isn't the most beloved of colors on its own, but designers like it because it reads as a neutral and pairs with nearly every other color. Further, when natural woods are used, brown retains the warmth associated with the natural world.

Try it out: Use some natural woods, place a fired ceramic sculpture on a shelf, work in cognac leather upholstery, or go big with dark brown velvet drapes.

WHITE

Attributes: Purity, simplicity, cleanliness, balance, clarity, openness, hope, emptiness

Impacts: White walls are associated with professionalism, which accounts for the many white walls in office buildings.[13] People who work in white offices report feeling less distracted.[14] White walls also make wall art and décor pop.

Try it out: Paint your home office a crisp but warm white, collect some functional ceramic or marble pieces (fruit bowl, anyone?), add a macramé wall hanging, get a bouclé accent chair.

Since every color carries its own energies, use them in concert with other favorites or supporting shades to make a room feel harmonious. We recognize this feeling when everything seems to fit together in a cohesive big picture.

Music is a great analogy for working with color. Just as single notes are specific sound waves, single colors represent their own vibration on the color spectrum. Each color adds its own note or tone, and each combination of colors creates a different "song" that conveys different tones and emotions. Colors can make a room feel energetic or calming, joyful or somber, and if colors are discordant, it makes for unpleasant visual noise.

This same idea is what designers mean when they talk about creating a unifying color story. All the colors used should complement each other and support the same mood, vibe, or visual palette. The rest of the chapter discusses what to consider when choosing colors for your own home. A great place to start exploring the world of color harmony is to visit online palette sites like colorpalettes.net.

LIMIT YOUR CHOICES

Trying to figure out a room's or a home's color story can feel overwhelming at first. As you begin, limit your choices by picking three to five colors that work nicely together. Here are some things to consider as you mix and match:

> **Neutrals:** Typically, have one neutral color, such as gray, taupe, beige, black, or some greens. Neutrals ground a space and allow other elements to do their thing.

Bold contrast colors: Pick one darker hue that is repeated throughout the space.

Accent colors: These are bright colors or bold patterns that "pop," drawing the eye. Gem tones are popular, like magenta or turquoise, as are bright warm colors like orange and red. When accent colors are objects, like pillows, they are easy to switch out.

Multicolored rainbows: One perfectly placed rainbow—on a rug, pillow, or lampshade—can make a perfect accent. If you are drawn to the rainbow, use colors with a similar saturation or intensity of color. A pastel rainbow will still feel cohesive.

PLACE-BASED COLOR VIBES

Another way to choose color palettes is to pick colors associated with a place you love. If you could be anywhere in the world, where would it be? Does Palm Springs speak to your soul? Reach for bubblegum pinks, royal blues, and tangerine. Prefer a Japanese spa? Combine forest greens, beiges, muted navies, and crisp linen. Every high-vibe place in the world has an associated color story.

Feeling ill at ease where you live now after a big move? Choose beloved colors that represent your new landscape. This can help you feel more connected to your life in the moment. You don't have to go all in on the prevailing regional color palette, but incorporating some of it into your décor can do wonders for making you feel more at home.

Sources of Color Inspiration

You can find inspiration for palettes and color stories almost anywhere. Use your intuition to decide what appeals to you. I often find inspiration in an object or a material, such as a rug or wallpaper, whose colors have already been pored over by professionals. For one thing, it's quicker, since you are building from the honed experience of people who work with color every day. Here are some of my favorite sources for color inspiration:

Fabric or wallpaper: Steal color combinations directly from a beloved Indian kantha throw, French tablecloth, classic American quilt, hand-painted serving platter, Turkish kilim pillow, or wallpaper—anything with at least five different colors.

Nature: Let the palette of a natural landscape spark your exploration. Or use materials like wood, rattan, and caning to add natural hues.

Rugs: Use more subdued versions of the colors in a bold, patterned rug.

Your wardrobe: Choose the colors that you (and your partner) wear most often.

Nostalgic places: Do you have fond memories of your grandparents and their historic home? Re-create their pink–tiled bathroom in your own.

Color psychology: Pick colors based on the vibe you want, using color psychology for guidance.

Artwork: Re-create the palette of a favorite artwork, adjusting the tones or pulling only the less-prominent colors.

Neutrals: For a calm space, use more subdued or neutral versions of your favorite colors.

Your personality: Ask your friends what color comes to mind when they think of you and choose that for an accent.

Finally, if you are also decorating a newly painted space, keep swatches of your color palette with you at all times. That way, whenever you go shopping, you can check possible purchases against your color story. Remember, items don't need to be exact color matches. If your general accent color is mustard, any items within the mustard family—from ochre to marigold—might be good choices.

FIND YOURSELF

What story do you want to tell through color in your home?

What's one small step you can take today to start your exploration with color?

10

MAKE SPATIAL CHANGES

D ecoration in the home often mirrors the wider culture. During the Enlightenment, European salons often had an entire wall of dramatic portraiture hung frame-to-frame. These rooms inspired people to absorb and integrate the new ideas of the time while sparking wide-ranging discussions about philosophy, morality, and aesthetics. In the sixteenth century, entire rooms were given over to cabinets of curiosities, called *Wunderkammer*. These collections of natural and human-made objects reflected the era's interest in scientific discovery and allowed wealthy people to display stories from their travels and confirm their social status. Meanwhile, the home of a nineteenth-century religious immigrant in America might have walls barren of decoration. This spoke to the person's interest in introspection and a profound desire to focus on their spiritual life, not the material world.

These days, anything goes with art and objects in the home. Our spaces more often reflect ourselves and might contain all these elements: gallery walls full of family photos or artworks, displayed collections that reflect our curiosities and intellectual interests, and pared-down spiritual spaces that foster calm reflection. Today, we get to play around with our spaces outside of societal expectations to determine exactly the right fit for us.

This chapter looks at a variety of issues related to home décor and arranging spaces to create the mood we want. This includes using negative space, maximalism versus minimalism, how to organize open spaces, and how to display artwork and collections.

The Quiet Power of Negative Space

As you find balance between the objects, furniture, and other elements in your home, pay close attention to negative space. Despite its name, it's a very good thing. Negative space refers to the undecorated background. It's the empty wall space behind pictures and art, or the unfilled areas on a bookshelf, those not occupied by books and objects.

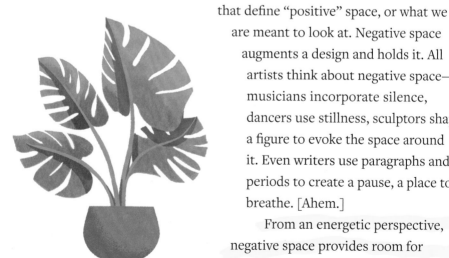

Negative space helps create boundaries that define "positive" space, or what we are meant to look at. Negative space augments a design and holds it. All artists think about negative space—musicians incorporate silence, dancers use stillness, sculptors shape a figure to evoke the space around it. Even writers use paragraphs and periods to create a pause, a place to breathe. [Ahem.]

From an energetic perspective, negative space provides room for energy to move. Clutter stops energy in its tracks, but negative space allows energy to swirl freely and even linger where you want. Some people thrive in environments packed with objects and visual stimuli, but most people need a balance of positive and negative spaces—places where something is going on and places where nothing is happening—to feel balanced. If your life feels out of balance, if you are stressed out, or if you are feeling stuck and bored, finding the right mix between positive and negative space should be your first course of action.

Maximalism Versus Minimalism

There is a recent home trend toward maximalism—that is, interiors with complex and evocative materials, abundant color, and lots of sensory input. Examples include velvet couches, gem tones, detailed large-scale wallpapers, oversized objects, animal imagery, and lots of rich texture. In other words, in a maximalist space, a lot is going on all at once—lots of visual stories, textures, patterns, and an array of shapes and styles. These spaces have visual complexity, but too much—or a high level of detail contained within someone's view—can be completely exhausting.

At the other end of the spectrum is minimalist design. Over the past decade, minimalism has become a popular choice in domestic spaces, which may reflect the sensory overload that the internet has brought into our lives. We spend so much time working on computers and engaged with the digital world, our eyes simply need a rest. As the name implies, a minimalist space is simpler, with fewer details, colors, and patterns, giving the eye less to consume and the brain less to digest. A minimalist room can feel like one big exhale that allows us to focus more completely on whatever needs our attention.

Minimalism and maximalism represent two design extremes that provide guideposts to work between. Most people fall somewhere in the middle. This is the sweet spot designers refer to as a balanced space. This is because many people thrive best in spaces that are mixed—ones that satisfy the human need for visual stimulation and engagement while also providing empty spaces to rest. Studies have found that too much visual complexity impedes our brain's ability to process.[15] On the other hand, not enough visual stimulation can be boring.

Experiment in your own home and find the right balance that works for you. If you feel overloaded, leave some walls blank, declutter shelves, or get rid of a few chairs. If life feels like it's a bit too much, dial back the color, remove half the objects on your mantel (or even all of them), or add some neutral colors. If you feel uninspired at home, add some patterns, hang vibrant art, or fill a wall with travel photos. Add some highly patterned or textured throw pillows, wallpaper a room in a bold paper, or change a boring light fixture to something more personal.

What works best might also change over time, and it can vary from room to room. If you feel a need for more excitement in your life, create more visual excitement in your home. If you or your child is having trouble focusing while working at home, reduce the amount of visual clutter in the space where you work. Have you grown tired of cooking? Spice up the kitchen with a new backsplash that adds shine, color, and pattern. You can use visuals to cue your behavior and create the right balance for you.

PERSONALITY QUIZ: ARE YOU INTROVERTED OR EXTROVERTED?

When making spatial shifts, it helps to be aware of your own personality and tendencies. Take this quick quiz to see whether you tend toward introversion or extroversion or are a balance of both. Check all the boxes that apply. Are you more one than the other?

INTROVERSION:

O I see alone time as quality time.

O I like people but feel drained after being in a crowd.

O I tend to be reflective and self-aware, with a running interior monologue.

O I seldom long to be the center of attention.

O I observe people and am a good listener.

EXTROVERSION:

O I love hosting, and it comes naturally to me.

O I seek out new experiences.

O I get bored when I'm alone.

O I like to process my feelings verbally with other people.

O I'm not fazed by loud sounds and crowded places, and I often enjoy them.

Introverts usually prefer a calm space, one that includes the following:

- Interior walls and defined spaces
- Subdued textures
- Less detail
- Scenes from nature
- Muted palettes
- Individual seating
- Personal space
- Fewer objects
- Blank space

Extroverts usually prefer an energized space, one that includes the following:

- Open floor plans
- Lush textures
- Rich detail
- Pictures of people
- Bold, saturated color
- Less personal space
- Personalized décor
- Multiple seats in one room
- Shared seating

Open floor plans can be overwhelming to live in, since being able to see everything at once in a living space can make you feel like the blazing eye of Sauron (of Lord of the Rings fame). Here are some designer tricks to organize and divide open spaces so your eyes and body have places to rest.

Create zones: Divide a larger space into smaller rooms or sitting areas. Add a dining area, position a seating area around a focal point, and put in overhead light fixtures to define the zones.

Pick your palette: Choose a cohesive color palette by picking three or four main colors and repeating them in upholstery and décor. Paint all the walls one color.

Float the furniture: Pull your largest pieces of furniture away from the walls to invite more flow. In small spaces, place a long couch with its back to an open area to define the space.

Anchor with rugs: Define a seating or dining area with the right-size rug.

Put plants to use: A large, leafy plant like a fiddle leaf fig or a snake plant can act as an energetic divider between larger zones.

Hang curtains: Floor-to-ceiling curtains artfully placed can provide more functionality in places where separation of spaces is difficult.

Raise a partition: A decorative screen or a giant see-through bookshelf can be a strong visual divider between zones. Black-framed glass doors are particularly of-the-moment, and a fireplace with two sides reads home and hearth like nothing else.

Play on personality: If cohesion feels too buttoned up, give two adjoining spaces radically different vibes.

Think curvy: If your space makes you feel boxed in, a curved sofa placed at a distance from a room's corners helps the eye move more freely.

Make a right angle: A corner sectional placed in the middle of a room clearly defines a hangout hub as its own room.

Improve focus: If it's hard to focus or pay attention in an open space, position some seating toward the least busy view.

Work the fifth wall: The ceiling is the so-called fifth wall. To help unify a room, use a single ceiling color or element, such as ceiling tiles, wood beams, paint color, or even a large-scale wallpaper.

Use statement objects: A single sculptural object can bring gravitas to a designated space. A range hood can draw the focus in the kitchen, a cool centerpiece can pull the energy to the table, and a patterned umbrella stand can steal the show at the front door.

Build a partition: For a permanent fix, hire a carpenter to fabricate a beautiful millwork partition to divide different zones.

Visual Art

My family owns a 1970s etching of a couple walking hand-in-hand with two other people stepping into and out of the frame. When I once asked my mom why she and my father had bought it, she said they were just drawn to it.

I always thought of it as a bleak display of how people come together, but how we always truly walk alone (dark, I know). My sister saw herself as both of the separate figures, one off in the distance forging ahead, while my mother and I held hands. It makes sense. I was always more clingy than she was, and she was the more independent one.

One day, my mother brought this monetarily valuable gift to my home to give to me. I was trepidatious. What kind of dark magic would this artwork—with its blanched-out palette, its grim energy—weave in my home?

Art does this to us—it invites us to bring to it our own perceptions and stories, our cultural backgrounds, our vast emotional landscapes, our hurts and joys. This can be both good and bad, depending on our reaction. Studies show that looking at something we perceive as beautiful improves brain function. Art can also situate us within the parts of our story we value most and reflect aspects of the human experience we celebrate and desire. When we choose to live with art, we are identifying states of being we want to experience day to day.

Or not. Art can be a real bummer if it evokes the wrong feelings. People sometimes put things on their walls that represent negative emotions or states: a bleak landscape that embodies loneliness, a busy abstract that provokes chaotic feelings, a sculpture of grief. Art can symbolize something we haven't moved on from or a wound we still pick at. And every day we pass it, its presence leaves an emotional imprint.

Identify your preferred states of being and consider any art currently on display in your home. Do they align? If not, go on a glorious search for a work of art that does. Choose artworks that carry the energies you want to embody in yourself.

Types of Art Energies

Whatever you display on your walls and shelves sends out energy with a specific vibration based on its materiality, provenance, and the meaning you attach to it. Don't display any art that you don't connect with or that doesn't elicit desired feelings.

Since my mood tends toward the melancholy, I prefer art that lifts my spirits. My favorite artworks resonate with curiosity, guidance, serenity, and even, dare I say, euphoria.

My husband, ever the rehabilitator, finds the greatest happiness in works that he has improved upon. When we bought a large painting in a thrift store, Adam repainted and hand-gilded the horrible frame. Now this art carries the special magic of the upcycled and his spirit lifts whenever he encounters it. In fact, most of the artworks in our home are thrifted and improved upon, as that pleases us both.

Here are some positive types of energy art can bring to the home.

Creation energy: Every piece of art was made by someone's hands and spirit. Collectors prize provenance, and you can, too, whether that's feeling attachment to an artist, the period in which the artist created the work, the place it was created, or the mediums used.

Acquisition energy: The way art comes into your life is its own story. Sometimes the story behind an acquisition is more interesting and fun than the artwork itself, and that's okay. So you went to Tijuana, had too many margaritas, and bought a kitschy dolphin sculpture. Now that dolphin commemorates the moments when you completely let go.

Aesthetic energy: The human eye appreciates art for its pure aesthetic value. If you don't know what you like, visit an art museum and take notes. Better yet, browse a local art fair. You're likely to find original art you can take home rather than making do with a Caravaggio print.

Symbolic energy: Art that is realistic or representational—that depicts recognizable people, places, and things—is explicitly symbolic. A path through the woods, a towering lighthouse, an island in a vast ocean, a sculpture of a hand: All these things can symbolize universal emotions and experiences we value. Whatever others say art symbolizes is less important than the meaning it holds for us. A vase filled with flowers is a celebration of life; empty on a shelf, it suggests a welcomeness to possibilities.

Emotional energy: Art is great at working the room when it comes to emotions—and not just the primal Pixar feelings of joy, fear, disgust, anger, and sadness, but the full spectrum. When considering bringing art into the home, the real question isn't "Do I like it?" but "How does it make me feel?"

Types of Art

When it comes to art, don't restrict yourself to flat, 2D media on your walls. There is a wide range of types to explore.

Paintings, drawings, and photos: Paintings, photography, and other 2D images have a high impact when hung on walls, plus they don't take up too much space and are easily moved around. It isn't difficult to acquire real, artist-made works on the cheap at vintage stores and flea markets. Go for authentic: Prints of works, even signed ones, never carry the same spirit and energy as a singular work made by hand.

Tapestries: Tapestries have made a bit of a design comeback in the last few years, but collectors have loved them for centuries. Whether woven or with painted images on fabric, they add great softness to a room while also providing large-scale impact. They can read as formal and historic, so balance them with newer items to avoid that museum vibe.

Wall hangings: Hooray for the rediscovered art of macramé and other woven crafts, which have become favorite décor objects in the past decade! The vast array of textured fabrics and textiles can cue us to remember the story of our soft, mortal selves and our desire for touch.

Sculpture: Many 3D décor objects share similar qualities with sculpture, but handmade artworks have a certain gravitas. If you don't have room for sculptures inside, look for an outdoor space, like a garden or front yard. Sculpture needs room to appreciate it. Or consider wall sculpture. Even a well-designed hat can become an object of aesthetic beauty when hung on the wall.

Mobiles: Hanging sculptures that move with the air are a form of kinetic art with enduring appeal, and the human eye loves to watch movement—hence their ubiquity above cribs. I like mobiles in spaces where there isn't much else going on, so you can let yourself watch, undistracted, as the artwork unfolds.

Emotionally Reframing Family Pieces

What do we do when we are the only one in the family who doesn't love a piece of art or when inherited objects have mixed associations for us? One possibility is to emotionally "reframe" them.

As for the etching my parents brought, I knew I had a choice. I actually liked it on an aesthetic level; it's a neat work. If I hadn't liked it at all—if I hated its colors or style—I would have cast it off without any issues whatsoever. So, while I had always seen it as a dark and gloomy depiction of divorce, I didn't have to continue viewing it that way. Much as a therapist might ask us to reframe a negative story about ourselves, I asked myself what else it could mean.

At the time, I was thinking a lot about mentors. In particular, I had a beloved childhood piano teacher, so I placed the etching above the piano, and every time I sat down to play, I thought of this person. Before long, the etching developed a whole new meaning for me—one of guidance and development.

You can do this with any artwork that is not working for you, particularly with family pieces others don't want to get rid of. Find a place where any less-than-favorite art pieces might make more sense or where their meaning can be rewritten.

Collections

When I was a travel writer, I decided I wanted to create a row of Cold War–era globes atop a built-in in my office. My husband and I began the slow curation of secondhand school globes until I had six of them, every one with the Eastern Bloc countries. Soon, friends were nabbing cheap globes wherever they saw them. I told myself they sent a strong message that I was legit. They reminded me of my childhood pride at being able to spell Czechoslovakia.

Collecting things is a physical expression of an emotional urge. Some collect to express loyalty to a school or sports team—to belong. Some collect for the prestige—to appear wealthy or to have higher status. Some collect celebrity objects to make other people's stories their own. Others seek the excitement of the hunt and the joy of discovery—they relive the stories every time they look at their collection.

Whatever your reason for collecting, buying something that fits your personality brings greater joy, according to a 2016 University of Cambridge study.[16] In other words, money *can* buy happiness, but only when you do you, boo. A collection has personal meaning, one based on your own associations, memories, aesthetic tastes, and urges. (Note that I'm not speaking here about the mental illness known as hoarding, which is something that should be addressed by an appropriate expert.) For most people, collecting is all about satisfying an emotional need that is expansive and never ends. We don't fall in love once, with one object; we seek that feeling again and again.

It's always instructive to consider the reasons why we collect what we collect. Sure, it's enough to say: "I like it." But enjoyment arises for a reason, and even the simplest collection carries meaning. For instance, a Pez dispenser collection might recall the joy of childhood, or it might be someone's way of participating in a community they enjoy (that is, other Pez collectors). Or the fascination might lie in the object itself—in this case, a toy figure whose head is thrown back to reveal hidden candy. Armchair psychologizing aside, it's worth considering the meaning of your own collection to decide how to display it in your home.

Collections Tend to Accumulate

Almost by definition, collectors want to grow their collections, but this can quickly run into a practical problem: Space within a home is valuable real estate. Collections have a way of taking over spaces, so consider carefully where to place yours, and pay very close attention to what feels like too much. Collectors often need two spaces: one for public display, and one for private display or storage.

Also, if you have a collection whose time has passed, be firm with family and friends. Let them know that you're done collecting so your collection doesn't keep growing when you don't want it to. While you don't have to get rid of a collection whose time has passed, I often recommend it, as it can be quite freeing. It is like casting off a former self. You can always store a collection in a place where you don't see it every day, but if it's still in your home, it retains energy in your life.

Ultimately, the goal is to find the right ratio of useful and beautiful things in a home. This issue has sent generations of couples to the therapist's couch, so if you have a partner, have regular conversations about it. Even just for yourself, check in regularly to determine whether the meaning and joy you get from your collection justifies the amount of living space you are devoting to it.

Collectors Like to Collect

Over time, I reconsidered my globe collection. In the first years of our young family, I traveled less. The globes became a daily reminder of all of the places I could no longer visit. I cared less about my own childhood fascinations than about my own children growing up right in front of me. I eventually donated all but one of my globes, and it was three years before I had the urge to collect anything again.

But I did get the urge, as many collectors do, so be thoughtful about what would reflect who you are now. When I was ready, I landed on the idea that I wanted to be more receptive to what was coming to me: people, opportunities, ideas. So I asked my mother for a Bucks County potato basket she and my dad bought for their first wedding anniversary, as well as my great-grandmother's handmade picnic basket. About a month later, my father sent me a picture of tiny baskets my grandmother had made. Now they reside in a front room of our home. This is where I want to be right now—open to whatever is coming my way, ready to carry it with me.

If you're ready for a new collection, give yourself time before collecting. Look for objects that come in a variety of incarnations and from different time periods. Hold objects in your hands to see how you respond. Consider how much space you have in your house, and in your life, for a new collection. For instance, if someone sews, a thimble collection takes up much less space than antique sewing machines. Think about what you'll feel every time you look at your growing collection. Enjoy the hunt.

Displaying Collections

Here is a list of ways for displaying different types of collections.

Art: Make a gallery wall of 2D pieces you love, be they paintings, drawings, or vinyl album covers.

Small items: Scour flea markets and vintage stores for old letterpress type cases or frame them all together in one display case.

Decorative plates: Hang them on the wall like art.

Medium-size objects: Anything too big for a wall but too small for an already full bookshelf can be placed on a narrow floating shelf.

Small 3D objects: Glass apothecary jars can contain small items while making them visible.

Larger 3D objects: Group hats, decorative plates, hand-painted tins, antique egg cups, air plant holders, elaborate Bundt pans, necklaces, and other 3D items in a cluster for a striking visual display.

Fabric: Hang scarves, beautiful fabrics, bandanas, or embroidered napkins on a line, but out of direct sunlight.

Books: In addition to organizing books alphabetically or by genre, consider visual interest. Perhaps group books by size or color.

FIND YOURSELF

✳

Is there space on your walls and in your rooms for new energy to move into your life?

How do the works of art in your home intersect with or support your story?

11

GROUND YOURSELF
WITH SCENT, TEXTURE,
AND ANIMAL ENERGY

One of my good friends is recently divorced, and she used reimagining her space as a way to move through that experience. Afterward, when I visited her home, I was amazed—she had redecorated, bought a new rug, started paying for cleaners, and rearranged the furniture in her main living space. A lightness hung in the air. I was in complete awe of how she was addressing the changes in her life.

She had also redone the bedroom. My friend and her ex-husband were and are people of strong Christian faith, and they had displayed a stunning collection of crosses from around the world on the largest bedroom wall. I was quite surprised to find this room was also completely realigned, and it now pulsed with vibrant energy. The crosses were gone, the bed was positioned with great charm on an angle, and on the wall was a framed picture of two swans floating on a serene pond. She had moved the painting, which was done by her mother, from their living room.

Swans are rich symbols of trust, loyalty, bonding, grace, beauty, and purity. They are an avian species that mate for life. That—and their heart-stopping beauty—is one reason they have been used prominently in weddings as symbols of fidelity and a shared path. Swans are a potent metaphor for the truths of marriage—so beautiful above the water, but feet constantly kicking under the surface to keep things moving with perceived serenity.

Why had she moved the swans into her bedroom, where she saw them every morning and night? Were they a reminder of the partnership and commitment she had lost? I counseled her to take them down, but she kept them there. After all, she decided that work was more about her connection to her mother.

Animal Obsessions

We are often drawn to animals outside of reason and regardless of what their animal symbology might mean. Most of us are attracted to animals instinctually. I grew up a sensitive kid in a home full of women, and I was drawn to elephants, who socialize in groups of females and are known to have deep emotional lives. My highly ambitious and driven son loves sloths, which are potent, furry examples for how to live in the moment. My best friend, a therapist, hangs a giant painting of a whale on her wall, a symbol of emotional healing, rebirth, and listening to your inner voice.

Become aware of your own emotional associations and connections with animals, and intentionally bring that energy into your home. Every culture attaches symbolism to animals, and you can choose the meaning that speaks to you, or make up your own. The same animal can mean

ANIMAL MEANINGS

Here is a list of animals that are used often in home décor, along with what they commonly symbolize. Most are considered good luck.

ANIMAL	MEANING
Tiger	Strength, confidence, courage, adventurousness, spirit
Elephant	Prosperity, power, memory, stability, longevity
Pig	Abundance, intelligence, ferocity, ambition, relentlessness
Cat	Elegance, independence, magic, serenity, luxury
Dog	Adaptability, loyalty, patience, protection, joy
Bird	Elevation, enlightenment, hope, wisdom, perspective
Chicken	Curiosity, tenacity, renewal, potential, divination
Rabbit	Wealth, rebirth, sensitivity, gentleness, haste
Butterfly	Rebirth, transformation, change, vulnerability, positivity
Dragon	Purpose, truth, humor, passion, success
Fox	Independence, playfulness, protection, alertness, cunning
Fish	Abundance, success, emotions, health, inventiveness
Monkey	Ingenuity, community, playfulness, fun, humor, mischief
Peacock	Royalty, passion, sophistication, pride, immortality
Owl	Wisdom, transformation, intuition, prophecy, protection
Unicorn	Purity, innocence, enchantment, healing, freedom
Wolf	Loyalty, family, friendship, teamwork, wildness

something different and unique to each person. The swans represented a good, positive message for my friend's life. The goal is to be intentional about your placement of animal energy and know what it means to you.

Bringing Animal Imagery into Your Home

Place an animal object in a room and it is sure to get attention. Here are some ways to do that.

Figurines: Small figures are inexpensive, charming reminders found in styles to suit every décor persuasion.

Sculptures: Larger sculptures carry more of the weight of that animal's energy. They are a bold, idiosyncratic statement and best used sparingly.

Textiles: Though they seem to go in and out of fashion, animal prints—like a cheetah pattern on a pillow—can read as stylish neutrals and envelop you in animal spirit.

Rugs: Something like a woven Tibetan tiger rug feeds the yearning without actually killing the beast.

Wallpaper: A bold, repeating wallpaper with animal details brings a repeated message into any space.

Paintings and art: Depictions of animals in paintings or other wall art can be moved around the home wherever they are needed most.

Actual animals: Adopting a pet is obviously not a décor decision, but animals do have a powerful impact. Meanwhile, an outdoor bird feeder is an excellent choice to encourage wildlife around your home.

The Message of Scent

Scent is personal, primal, emotional, evocative, and most importantly, true fun. Today, we know more about our mysterious sense of smell than ever before, and each year brings new studies about how scent guides our behaviors, feelings, and thoughts. Scent plays a role in how we experience life's most heightened moments: pleasure, ecstasy, joy, love, comfort, even grace. Thus, in our homes, we can use scent to cue emotions and the messages we tell ourselves.

That said, most of the time, we can't smell our home, the same way we usually can't smell ourselves. Our nose is too attuned to our scent to be aware of it. Our olfactory receptors, in a process called olfactory adaptation, filter out known smells to focus on whatever is novel or might indicate danger. In other words, if your home had its own perfume, it would be called "Safety."

But layering scent on top of your home's existing olfactory vibe is an adventure in sensuality, and it's well worth the effort, whether you are a person who likes to walk in their own cloud of perfume or you run past beauty counters with your nose pinched. In fact, my favorite people to work with are those who don't identify as a fragrance person.

By adding scent to the home, you enter a world of primal experience. You signal to yourself to be more fully alive in your own body. Scent—which is intimately connected to the breath—brings us into the present moment. This is certainly one reason why religious rituals have used it for millennia. This section guides you in discovering what scents you like best and how to work them into rituals that honor your space.

A Stinky House Repels Good Energy

A client of mine recently bought her first home, a fixer. Its previous inhabitants had been smokers, and the stench of acrid tobacco had leached into all of the home's rooms. What to do?

For large-scale house funk, a professional deep clean helps immensely. But for a fresh canvas, paint the walls with a primer designed to block out stains and smells, like KILZ. This also makes walls less porous, so they are less likely to absorb smells. Here are some other great methods for removing unwanted scents:

- Shake baking soda into carpets and upholstery, leave for two hours, and then vacuum it up.
- Change the air filter for your home on a regular schedule.
- Open windows daily.
- Run a lemon (cut into chunks) through your garbage disposal.

Bringing Scent into the Home

Here are some ways to layer fragrance in the home. However, be aware: Less is always more with fragrance. Don't overdo it, and think about how all of the occupants in your home will respond. Animals also respond to scent, and cats and dogs both tend to dislike citrus scents like lemon, orange, and lime.

One common way to add scent at home is to use candles, but not all candles are the same. Consider how the candle is made.

- Choose one made from all-natural ingredients, such as soy-based, coconut oil, or beeswax. Avoid paraffin.
- Look for a long burn time.
- Seek candles with two or three scents using 100 percent natural essential oils.

Here is a list of scent suggestions by room of the house:

Bedroom: My favorite scents for the bedroom are something anyone sleeping in the room would feel comfortable wearing on their bodies. If you want to improve sleep, choose a soporific oil like lavender, chamomile, jasmine, or geranium. To foster romance or self-love, try sandalwood, ylang ylang, rose, vetiver, or anything you'd want to smell on a lover.

Kitchen: Scents made for the kitchen should not compete with what is cooking on the stove. Indeed, if you make a ritual of simmering fragrant herbs with citrus fruit, you can give your house's most important space a lingering freshness. To add a diffuse scent, look for scents you enjoy in cooking—orange, rosemary, oregano, basil, peppermint, or lemon, which most people associate with cleanliness.

Office: Any scents that increase alertness, boost creativity, or otherwise improve cognitive function do well in an office. Bring in candles or diffuse rosemary, vetiver, lemon, citrus, pine, or ginger.

Living room: In any place where coziness is called for, look for scents with added resonant warmth, like amber, cardamom, cedarwood, black pepper, cinnamon, or ginger. Fruity notes like fig and passion fruit provide a "home sweet home" vibe, but in an open living space, be careful that they don't compete with the kitchen.

Laundry room: Lavender is the classic choice for laundry—its etymology comes from the Latin *lavare*, meaning "to wash." Put sachets in your drying cycle or use a naturally scented detergent. If lavender is an allergen for you, try cedar and sage as modern updates.

ONLY THE ESSENTIALS: OILS FOR THE HOME

With an aromatherapy diffuser, you can choose which essential oils to layer. Scent is quite personal, and people can respond to the same scent very differently, based on their own memories and cultural associations. Here is a good primer for which feelings or states of mind are cued by which scents, but let your own experience be your guide.

Uplifting: Citrus scents like lemon, orange, grapefruit, bergamot, lime, tangerine, citronella, lemongrass, mandarin

Calming: Florals like chamomile, geranium, jasmine, lavender, neroli, rose, rosewood, ylang ylang, petitgrain

Balancing: Herbals like chamomile, angelica root, clary sage, fennel, melissa, rosemary, thyme, oregano

Medicinal: Camphor-related scents like cajeput, eucalyptus, pennyroyal, laurel leaf, lavandin

Clarifying: Mints like spearmint, wintergreen, peppermint

Warming: Spices like aniseed, basil, black pepper, cardamom, cinnamon, coriander, cumin, ginger, nutmeg, cassia, clove

Grounding: Resinous scents like benzoin, elemi, frankincense, myrrh, Peru balsam

Centering and stabilizing: Woody scents like cypress, juniper berry, pine, sandalwood, fir, cedarwood, palo santo, rosewood, patchouli, vetiver

Texture Feels Good

We have a deep, human craving to feel at home in our bodies, and our sense of touch helps provide this. In recent years, we have wanted to feel soothed at home, and this has sparked a golden age of texture. Textured products are showing up everywhere: as nubby macramé wall hangings, rough artisan vases, frosted glass vessels, bumpy rattan baskets, smooth wood beads, fringy light pendants, and so on. I, for one, am so thankful for this. The ultimate beauty of texture is how it balances out what I like to call the tyranny of the visual—a world in which we live on, with, and through our screens.

Recent research has expanded what we know about our sense of touch and how it relates to our emotions. First, our sense of touch is so acute we are like touch machines. Touch sensors on our skin are about half a millimeter apart, and yet we can sense textures down to tens of nanometers. One study identified twenty separate dimensions of texture—that's an entire world of sensation we can play with in our home.[17] Of course, some textures are more inviting than others—we love to run our palms over velvet and fur but not a sharp cactus. In fact, studies show that we associate different textures with different emotions.[18] Negative moods lead us to crave touch—in the form of hugs or cradling a body pillow.[19] And the natural materials that most often cause happiness are fur, wood, silk, leather, and velvet.

As with color, each person responds differently to different textures. Notice when you are drawn to certain finishes and textures. Pay conscious attention to how surfaces and sensations make you feel on an energetic level. Then, if a texture feels good or elicits a positive quality, bring it into your home to add balance to your life. Ideally, shop at brick-and-mortar stores, so you can touch objects before you purchase.

Designers love texture because it helps them balance a room, make it more engaging, and enhance the experience of the homeowner. Mixing textures expertly requires lots of practice, but you can also trust your instincts. If something feels good, literally and emotionally, it rarely fails. Here are some tips to remember about texture.

Contrast: Contrasting textures allow certain objects in the room to stand out. Imagine the difference between a thick-knit throw and a smooth, cashmere one.

Mixing: Consider the mix of textures and finishes you want by first experimenting with a physical mood board. Consider what mixes work best before making it manifest.

Balance: Nothing in excess. This is never more true than with texture. Too much can completely overwhelm a space, as can too much of the same texture.

Space: Rooms with finished textured walls are perceived to be significantly smaller than rooms with no texture.[20]

Reflection: Texture can reflect or swallow light. Darker, heavier objects swallow more light; patterns often reflect it.

Layering: Even a visually monochromatic room can work if it uses contrasting textures. The trick is to use the same texture multiple times in one room to make it feel cohesive.

Favorite combos: Sometimes, certain design styles and eras are defined by a particular mix of finishes and textures. The modern farmhouse style, for example, is usually an enchanting mix of flat neutral colors and worn metals (think oil-rubbed bronze) along with natural textures like linen and wood paneling. If you like that style, copy those texture combinations, or mimic the mix of finishes used by designers you admire.

TOUCHABLE TEXTURE

Expand the range of textures in your spaces by going deeper with the possibilities.

SOFT

Materials: Cotton, mohair, wool, velvet, denim, corduroy

Where to use: Sheets, pillows, rugs, upholstery, draperies

CRISP

Materials: Paper, plants, cotton, flowers

Where to use: Sheets, light fixtures, books, sculpture, wall art

NUBBY

Materials: Fringe, macramé, bouclé, embroidery, chenille, big knit, corduroy

Where to use: Wall hangings, pillows, upholstery, artwork, blankets, wall coverings, rugs, lampshades

FURRY

Materials: Fur (fake preferred), sheepskin, Tibetan lambswool

Where to use: Throws, pillows, rugs, petting your animals

RICH

Materials: Velvet, jacquard, brocade, silk, carved wood

Where to use: Upholstery, napkins, pillows, draperies, wall hangings, objects

SHINY

Materials: Metal, mirror, marble, glass, ceramics

Where to use: Hardware, mirrors, objects, lighting, seating, lamps, tile

WARM

Materials: Wood, ceramics, linen, cotton

Where to use: Furniture, surfaces, architectural accents, pillows, objects, wall panels

ROUGH

Materials: Metal, jute, rattan, rope, branches, cane, concrete, seagrass

Where to use: Furniture, rugs, surfaces, artwork, accents

Go Texture Shopping

If you are a novice to texture, get ready—it's time to go texture shopping! On a free day, visit one of your favorite home stores with the sole purpose of seeing how you respond to different textures. Hold objects in your hands to see if you feel an energy exchange. Rub your hands along the throws or squeeze a knob on a showroom bookshelf. Take your time and note what you love and what is an absolute no. Don't even think about whether or not something is right for you or your home. Focus purely on texture. The more you dial in your own taste, and identify the materials that feel good to you, the more that material will begin showing up when you aren't even looking for it.

FIND YOURSELF

What animals are you drawn to? Does their symbolic meaning align with who you want to be?

What scents and textures do you gravitate toward and have the most positive associations for you?

12

INSPIRE DEEP WORK

U p until now, we haven't talked about the function of specific spaces in the home. But the spaces where we work matter—a lot. This chapter explores how to turn your work space into a great collaborator in your quest to do what gives your life purpose. This is particularly important if you find yourself distracted or stuck, if you've hit one of those proverbial brick walls, or if you just need a change of perspective. Addressing your work space is the first step toward shifting your energy and accomplishing the goals that matter most.

Years ago, before I started writing, I attended author readings and book signings, hoping that they might illuminate the writing path for me. Inevitably, during the Q&A, someone would ask about the writing process itself. The questions differed, but the gist was always the same: "How did you do it?"

When it comes to creativity, no maps or instruction manuals exist. But all creativity happens in a place, and that place can help or hinder us. In fact, many famous creatives are associated with the place where lightning struck: Jackson Pollack had his Sag Harbor cottage; J. K. Rowling had her perfect coffee shop; Steve Jobs had his garage. We can't copy others, but we can create the perfect place to support our own creative needs. Below, I provide a mix of ancient design principles and modern design theories that are all worth playing around with to find what works for you.

Identify Your Deep Work

To me, the term *deep work* refers to two things: doing work that is personally meaningful, that lights us up and fulfills our sense of life purpose; and also working deeply, with undistracted focus and passion. When we become deeply immersed in work that embodies our highest self, time stops. We enter a flow state so powerful that the rest of the world disappears. This is my absolute favorite place to be, when everything else just falls away and I feel the alignment of purpose and activity, the union of inspiration and action.

Creating the conditions for long periods of uninterrupted creative work is the subject of Cal Newport's popular book *Deep Work*, the tenets of which I apply to spaces. Right now, consider your own experiences working at home, whether that's in a dedicated office, in the garage, or at the dining room table. Do you frequently become distracted by all the other nagging needs of your life? What might be the ideal conditions that would allow you to devote longer stretches of time to your most important personal and work projects? Making changes to create those conditions helps us finish projects, make greater innovative leaps, and accomplish what we want.

For me, practically speaking, deep work means longer periods of uninterrupted time focused on my work and ensconced in a flow state.

Not days, not weeks, but stretches of at least three hours when I can really dig in. What undermines deep work is when I find myself toggling back and forth between activities like checking email, doing laundry, answering phone calls, and any distraction that pulls me out of the flow state.

Before addressing your space, however, take a moment to think about the other meaning of deep work. What work are you passionate about? What gives your life meaning and purpose? What do you want to achieve or accomplish? Focus less on specific accomplishments—like fame, fortune, or writing a bestseller—than on the meaningful activities you would like to fill your days. Take a few minutes and write down what deeper work looks like for you, then keep this in mind as you consider how to improve your work space.

Evaluate Your Work Space

Look around your office or work space right now and ask yourself: What message is my space telling me about my work?

Is it an old, unhelpful story about what kind of creator or worker you are? Or is it telling you someone else's story about what creativity and productivity require? Are there ways that this space undermines your flow state?

In the rest of this chapter, I focus mostly on office-type work spaces and desks. Of course, for some people, their important work happens in the kitchen or outside in the garden. It might happen at a workbench or in the driveway. If that is the case for you, simply translate these principles and examples to your situation.

However, in addition to all the other places important work can happen, many people also work at desks, so take a look at where yours is situated. How much space do you have to work in? Notice that your work

space isn't just a desk or a counter but the entire space you move in while working. Where is the energy of "work" situated in the room? Visualize every area associated with your work space as having energetic boundaries. What does this include beyond your desk? This visualization is particularly important for people who work remotely at home for their full-time job.

At this point, you might be anticipating me to say, "If you want to foster creativity, you need a clean desk." I've had some people pipe up, "Hey, I'm a messy creative! I thrive in messes, and I only feel good when I am surrounded by all of my materials!" And if you're that person, someone who genuinely thrives off of messes, I'm not going to ask you to change or be a different person. In fact, the whole point is to identify what helps you be your best creative self: making connections between disparate ideas, finding solutions that others have missed. What I'd like you to do, though, is examine your current habits and work space and think about ways to improve it. And if you're someone who often struggles with organization, then tidying your office or work space is one way to rewrite that story. What's important is discovering what works for you and then sticking to it.

With that in mind, here are three important areas to consider: lighting, desk position, and how to deal with unfinished projects.

Adequate Lighting

I am friends with a couple who spent three decades working as engineers in a mile-long windowless facility. When they retired, they built a custom home with floor-to-ceiling windows on top of a hill where they would have full access to the entire path of the sun as it crosses the sky. They often joke about overcompensating, but I think their bodies knew exactly what they needed—enough light to make up for three decades of deprivation!

Light is energy, and energy is what we want flowing into all areas of our work life. Light has long been associated with inspiration, innovation, intellectual thought, and bringing order out of chaos. When we have insight, we are said to "shed light" on a problem.

If you are lucky enough to have a work space with abundant natural light, be thankful. Higher levels of natural light have been linked to more positive health outcomes like lower blood pressure, more restorative sleep, better academic performance, better eyesight over time, and a host of other benefits.[21]

Evaluate the light in your work space right now and consider ways to bring more light in and, as designers say, brighten things up. Some ways to do this include removing heavy drapery or blinds, giving your room a good dusting (dust tends to swallow light), using paints that have a reflective sheen (I like a semigloss on bookshelves, for example), painting your room with lighter colors (which are more reflective), and employing mirrors (see "All Mirrors Are Magical," page 137).

LIGHTBULB MOMENTS

We are so attuned to the cultural image of a lightbulb signifying a burst of inspiration that even seeing a lightbulb turned on is enough to improve spatial, verbal, and mathematical reasoning.[22] Since this news appeared, more and more lighting designers have developed desk lamps and other lighting solutions with completely exposed lightbulbs. I have one in my own office. I turn it on at the beginning of a work session and switch it off when my work is over.

Layer Your Lighting

In an architectural space, there are three main types of lighting: ambient lighting, task lighting, and accent lighting. No single source of light can meet all of our lighting needs, which is why designers often talk about "layering" in their lighting plan.

Ambient lighting: This is the lighting that lights up the entire room, and it includes chandeliers, wall-mounted fixtures, track lights, table lamps, and floor lamps.

Task lighting: This includes desk lamps, pendant lighting over tables, under-cabinet lighting, and recessed fixtures. I don't always recommend splurging, but when it comes to switching on your work space desk lamp, buy yourself the most fabulous, beautiful, appropriately styled desk lamp. It could change how you feel about getting to work when you switch it on.

Accent lighting: Accent lights draw attention to specific areas or objects, and this has the magical effect of making a room appear larger. They can highlight an architectural feature, a painting or hung photograph, a collection of objects, or plants.

Productive Desk Placement

As furniture goes, desks are a relatively recent phenomenon. Our concept of a desk didn't come into fruition until 1797 (in the form of the French bureau), and the actual construction, look, and function has continued to evolve to suit our needs.

One thing hasn't changed: Desks are the command center. They are not necessarily the place where all of our creativity happens—I suspect that far greater breakthroughs happen in the shower—but they signal to our mind: *I am at work.*

In classical feng shui, desk placement continues to be one of the most important considerations for the office, whether it's at home or at work. Feng shui holds that desks should always be placed in the "command position," which is facing the room, with a view of the door, and preferably with a wall behind you. The reasoning is both protective and symbolic. If you are facing the door, you can see what's coming at you, and you also have the desk functioning as a protective force. If you've never experienced the empowering effects of a desk placed in the command position, I suggest you try it out.

That said, I'm constantly playing around with my desk position to discover how it affects me and my work. Originally, I had a desk facing the wall. If you face a wall, you might always feel like you are up against a wall in your work. The visual story is that you're hitting your head against the wall, like you're going nowhere. So I moved my desk around to face the door, and I placed the desk on an angle.

I kept it like this for a while, until I realized that when I walked in my home's front door, the first thing I saw was my desk. I constantly felt like I was working. I needed better work/life boundaries, and I needed to be able to shut off, so I moved my desk to a position still facing the entrance of the room but not visible immediately upon entering the front door.

ALL MIRRORS ARE MAGICAL

In feng shui, mirrors are often employed to create double views, to make a space feel larger, to reflect light, and to symbolically expand the purpose and meaning of a space. Avoid hanging a mirror facing your desk, since its effect is often to double your work load, but placing a mirror behind you can serve to ward off bad energy. Since mirrors represent wisdom and introspection, it might be just the right addition to your work space. But make sure your mirror is not cloudy, broken, divided into pieces, or one that has unfinished edges. These kinds of mirrors have foul consequences for humans, as they provide a distorted image of reality.

In my work as a magazine editor, I often see images of home offices where every accommodation has been made for the aesthetics—does it look good on the page?—with very little consideration of the actual work being done. Quite a few of these images have desks facing a wall or a window. Some people truly love looking out a window on a beautiful view while they work. Others naturally set up their desks to face a wall because that's what accommodates their desk in a smaller space. Both are fine choices when you are generating work that is more interior in nature, that isn't necessarily ready or intended for public consumption, or when you are working through a specific problem. But when you are ready to face the world with your work, to have impact and to have success in your chosen field, don't look out the window at what other people are doing. Face your desk toward the door, with your back against the wall.

When we think about the people we admire, both those living now and from history, we often see ourselves as fans. We sit at the feet of greatness. What if the opposite were true? What if all of the great humans we admire were actually fans of *our* work? What if they wanted to move *us* to do great things?

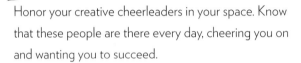

Honor your creative cheerleaders in your space. Know that these people are there every day, cheering you on and wanting you to succeed.

Books: Dedicate one shelf to the minds who have had the greatest influence on your personal development and on your work. Discrete rows of the influential books in your life is a wonderful way to create your own cheering section.

Busts: Sculptural portraits of admired people is a whimsical, fun way to bring inspiring stories and influential thought into a space. If the classical white-marble look feels off, paint them. No one said a bust of Joan of Arc has to be white.

Mood board: Cork boards offer flexibility and the tactile pleasure of shuffling and pinning, one of life's greatest pleasures. Sometimes we are moved more by the work, not the creator, so make a collage of works that you can view from your work space.

Frame them: If a cheerleader's work is more ethereal, as it is with music, consider how to honor it visually. You could frame an album cover (or several), or frame individual concert tickets from an important period of your life.

Display them: Sometimes a product tells an entire story unto itself. You can connect to someone whose work you admire by displaying it on your shelf or desk. For instance, an architect might display a tiny replica of Mies van der Rohe's Barcelona chair.

What to Do with Unfinished Projects

A Chinese proverb holds that once we've made it 90 percent down a path, we are halfway to our destination. This mathematical impossibility could explain why people tend to start so many creative projects but only finish a few. Today, software developers speak of the last 10 percent being the most difficult of any project. The lesson is clear: Finishing is monumentally hard. It is much easier to start a project, with all the vim, vigor, and fresh energy of new beginnings, than to stick with it to completion.

When is a project truly done? Projects are complete when we take an action to get them out in the world. If we leave unfinished work in our space and move on to something else, it will always be a drain on our creative energy. Unfinished projects nag at our spirit like a small child needing attention. Even worse, they affect the story we are telling ourselves: *I am someone who starts projects and doesn't finish them.*

If you find yourself leaving projects uncompleted, you can rework your space to help you become a closer. At the very least, you can make some adjustments in order to focus on the big, beautiful projects you'd like to bring to fruition.

Set aside some time to evaluate your unfinished projects. If these are physical projects, gather them together and assess them one by one. Ask: Does this project have the same vital energy it had when I was deep in the throes of working on it?

Then, you basically have three choices of what to do with an unfinished project: Finish it. Discard it. Store it elsewhere.

FINISH YOUR PROJECT

If, when you encounter a still-in-progress work that you had set aside and it still brims with the energy of creativity for you, you should make a conscious effort to finish it. Finished works build confidence and help solidify our identities as creators—whatever the medium. In finishing, we are also teaching ourselves a valuable lesson in what our own definition of "finished" looks like.

DISCARD YOUR PROJECT

What would it be like to get rid of a project that is unfinished? For me, it always feels a bit painful in the moment, but it is freeing in the long term. Letting go of unfinished work usually includes forgiving myself for what I have failed to finish. Accept that the time you spent on this project happened and that it has already given you whatever you needed from it.

By discarding a project, you won't hear its nagging voice, and it will be easier to focus on new, current projects. It doesn't matter if you can't physically see a project. If it is stored in your work space, it commands a certain presence, and it will always emit its own energies and ask for attention from you. For physical objects—sweaters that didn't get knitted, drawings half-drawn, sculptures that never got fired, letters never sent—physically discard them or throw them away. Digital work may not take up physical space and is easy to "hide," but consider storing files far from your current work, and ideally not on your desktop computer.

STORE YOUR PROJECTS

The urge to store unfinished projects can be strong. What will future generations need when they go searching for your personal archive to glean deep insights into human existence? How do you account for the time you spent on a project if there isn't any proof of the effort?

All snarkiness aside, the most important project you have is the one you are working on right now. If you must store your lifeless projects, make sure you put them as far away from your work space as possible. Put physical objects in another room—like a basement or an attic—and put digital files in the cloud or backed up on a separate hard drive. Then you know files reside somewhere, but you won't run across them unless you deliberately seek them out.

FIND YOURSELF

What could you add or take away from your designated work space in order to value your work more in your home?

Pull up your calendar: Pick a longer stretch of existing time and designate a good one to two hours to your most important work— the thing that makes you come most alive.

DESIRE

BRING YOUR ASPIRATIONS INTO YOUR SPACE

13

MAP your HOME'S ENERGY CENTERS

To really design a life, we have to take a top-down, big-picture view. A to-scale floor plan depicts how the various spaces of a house are divided up into functional spaces, but to add a layer of discovery, I use the feng shui bagua, or energy map, which is one of my favorite tools for shaping life intentionally at home.

What is it? The bagua (meaning "eight areas") is an eight-sided diagram that maps how vital energy moves through spaces and, in turn, through our lives. It originated as part of the I Ching (*The Book of Changes*) as a divination tool alongside Taoist astrology and the principles of yin and yang. This tool has been used regularly ever since as a practical way to bring balance and harmony to spaces.

Homes in the West generally respond well to square energy maps, which align with the traditional bagua but add a ninth area at the center. Each of these nine areas of the home corresponds to a different aspect of human life. Within these areas, we are symbolically working on that corresponding area of our life. The rub is that the areas correspond directly to our home's spaces regardless of their designated function. For example, a bathroom might reside in the area of the home corresponding to love and marriage, or a bedroom in the travel section.

The energy map takes amorphous, big-picture desires and gives them a physical place we can work with. When we devote time to working on an area of our energy map, knowing that we are assessing, adjusting, and reimagining a corresponding area of our life gives us a comforting level of agency. Life no longer happens to us. Instead, we become empowered to notice the things that need to be changed and to respond creatively to life's struggles. Small adjustments create big thrills, and bigger adjustments can change our life.

This book's fourth part, "Desire," is devoted to explaining and helping you use the energy map in your home. This chapter describes how the energy map works, and the next chapters explore each of the corresponding desires and how to use spatial solutions to activate those energies.

How the Energy Map Works

Why does changing something in one area of your home correspond with shifting energy in that part of your life? To be honest, I am not an expert in the mysteries of the I Ching. Years ago, I was curious about energy maps, and a feng shui practitioner told me: "You don't need to know how the bagua works to know that it works." Maybe so. Initially, I certainly used it with something amounting to blind faith before deciding it was for me. Now, after years of working with it, I have some theories of why it is effective beyond my belief in magic and manifestation.

The energy map gives people a physical home to locate their amorphous human wants. Western cultures have long promoted the elusive goal of creating a work/life balance, but finding the right way to direct our energies and attention in our actual lives is very complicated. The map gives us a physical space to send us messages in whatever area we feel is lacking in our life or whatever aspect we want to accentuate. Each part of the map is an opportunity to tell the story of that part of our life.

Nuance is called for, however. Just because a room corresponds with influence, that doesn't mean we should plaster the walls there with images of our face à la Andy Warhol. An online site might say to put a neon heart sign in our love and marriage center, but if we don't love neon hearts, it won't work. The goal is to develop our own personal symbology, so that when we want to activate a specific part of our life, we can call on materials, images, and objects that connect with those desires.

One of my favorite things about the energy map is how it allows us to dance with change, especially unexpected change. Often, life throws something at us that doesn't suggest a clear response or solution. Instead of quivering in fear or defeat, an effective means of coping is to use the energy map to identify the related area, and then declutter, move some objects around, switch up some imagery, change some messaging, or even just spend time in the corresponding part of our home.

Note that for each of the energy centers I have made suggestions about which forms, colors, and materials are considered to be most auspicious for these sections. You can always work based on your own symbology and storytelling, but if you want to play with feng shui, you

THE NINE ASPECTS OF THE ENERGY MAP

The energy map usually appears either as a square or an octagon, and this is laid over the first floor of the home, with the bottom of the map lined up with the front door. Each section corresponds to a different aspect of our lives.

CAREER AND LIFE PATH

 This is often where energy enters the home, front and center, the place of welcome, so changes made to this area will shape the challenges and successes you face in your career as well as your overall ability to welcome good change into your life.

WISDOM AND SELF-KNOWLEDGE

 Set to the left of the front of the home, this area is where your image of yourself and your state of wisdom and knowledge gathers and renews itself. Making alterations here can help you feel more confident in your choices, increase knowledge, and call more powerfully on your inner voice.

FAMILY AND ANCESTORS

 At the left middle of your floor plan resides your center for family and ancestors. Here is the best place to honor your connection to those who have come before you, to celebrate your bio or chosen family, and in general to feel deep connection to your people.

WEALTH AND PROSPERITY

 A steady flow of income into the home lifts everyone in the household, so activate this area whenever you want to increase feelings of wealth and prosperity or are just seeking more financial stability.

INFLUENCE, OR FAME AND REPUTATION

 Sharing ideas, having a great reputation in your community, and holding sway when it matters—these energies take up the area often referred to as "fame and reputation," but which I call "influence." Work here when you want your light to shine a little brighter.

LOVE AND PARTNERSHIP

 The energies of romantic relationships, marriage, committed partnerships, and self-love converge in the back right corner of the home. Activate this area if you want to deepen a relationship, start a new one, or just feel the warm embrace of loving yourself.

CREATIVITY AND CHILDREN

 The right middle section of the energy map captures the swirling energies of children and the spirit of abundant creativity. Start here if you are looking for a lighter heart, support for existing children in your household, or a surge of creative moxie.

TRAVEL AND HELPFUL PEOPLE

 Connect to people and places beyond your home life in this energy center, located at the front right of the map. It's a great place to support taking trips big and small and to call on the people whose presence is most helpful in your life.

SPIRITUALITY AND WELL-BEING

 The very center of the home connects with your essence as a spiritual being and your overall sense of physical health. Think of it as your mind-body space and attend to it for greater overall feelings of wellness.

could try employing colors and materials believed to enhance these centers. What pleases you matters most. In other words, if you learn that black is an auspicious color at the front door, you don't necessarily have to see your red door and paint it black. Maybe you just use oil-rubbed bronze house numbers.

Personal Struggles Often Relate to Spatial Struggles

When I speak with clients about areas of life they are struggling with, there often seems to be a corresponding spatial struggle that relates to their energy map. For example, if a woman is unhappy within her marriage, I might find that the area of the home associated with partnership has been given over completely to the husband's workshop. A scholar might be struggling for recognition, and I'll discover that the fame and reputation area is located in a bathroom. A single mom will tell me her children have taken over her entire life, and I'll find the front door opens directly onto a staircase heading up to the children's bedrooms. Houses aren't problems in and of themselves, but if they are affecting their homeowners in negative ways, they are calling out to be adjusted through energy enhancements and shifts in design.

Have you ever had a problem that just didn't seem fixable? That's because problems that reside in our heads tend not to get fixed until there is a corresponding worldly exchange. We don't heal a relationship with a person until we have spoken to that person. We don't feel appreciated by our work supervisors until we experience the energetic exchange of verbal praise or a promotion. We feel more comforted in times of grief when someone shows up to witness it. There is a very real connection between the way we grow and change and the energies we receive from others and from the spaces we inhabit.

Sometimes people ask me what happens if they have an issue that doesn't correspond to any of the energy map sections. However, I've never run into an issue that isn't connected or related to one of the nine realms. In fact, more than one area often relates. A desire for more human connection could relate to romantic partnerships, to children, to family, and/or to helpful people. A desire for a better job might relate to career, to money, to reputation, and/or to wisdom and self-knowledge. This is one of the benefits of the energy map: It's flexible, not reductive.

Draw Your Energy Map

As best as you can, draw the floor plan of the first floor of your home or apartment. If you have an existing, to-scale floor plan, reproduce that at a workable size.

Then superimpose the energy map over the drawing of the floor plan, aligning the bottom of the energy map with your front door. Ideally, the floor plan will be a rough rectangle or square, which you divide into thirds; make the nine squares roughly equivalent in size. Add the labels for each square on the energy map, starting with "career and life path" at the front door, and proceeding clockwise per the section descriptions above.

Of course, most homes are not neat boxes. If your home is an odd or elongated shape, adjust the extents of the energy map so that it covers the entire home, while trying to keep each section close to the same size. Below, I've included a floor plan and an energy map of my home's first and second floors to show how to make adjustments.

Further, since many houses are not square, you might also notice that there are areas of your house where it looks like you are missing part of the energy map. For my house, we are missing part of our travel and helpful people area. Though these sections exist outside the home, they are still part of your energy map. It just means that you have what is called a "missing corner" and should create a symbolic enhancement to fill in that area. For our home, we built a front porch in order to enhance our identities as people of service who wanted to connect with others in our neighborhood. You will hear some other examples later on about how my clients have identified and filled in their missing corners.

You might be surprised at first to see that the area of your home given over to these energy centers isn't associated with their function. The main bedroom might be located in the travel and helpful people corner; an office might be in love and partnership. That's okay. Wherever the energy centers align with your home's floor plan is

FIRST FLOOR   **SECOND FLOOR**

where they align. The point is to identify where the various energies of your life accumulate, so you know which part of your home needs change when related issues arise.

In the next nine chapters of this part, I discuss each of the nine energy centers and how smaller desires and problems relate to the big-picture aspirations that give your life a feeling of overall alignment. For instance, if you want a new car, that's not really about the car. What do you want the car for? To travel, to commute to a new job, to project a certain image? Using the energy map, you can help use your space to identify your actual needs and make changes within the home to support them.

FIND YOURSELF

What areas of the physical home are calling out to be improved?
Do you notice a connection to that area of
your life on your energy map?

What areas of your home feel good to you? Do you notice a
connection to that area of your life on your energy map?

14

ALIGN your CAREER
and LIFE PATH

he area in the center front of your home corresponds to your life path and career, so it's a perfect place to make adjustments or enhancements if you are looking to boost how you view your life, for big changes in your work situation, or to welcome new opportunities and energies.

A Magical Threshold for Energy

Many homes situate their main doors front and center, making it the absolute first place to start in any home energy project. Doors are thresholds—magical, transitional spaces. You're a different person once you walk through a door, which is one reason doors hold such rich potential for metaphor in our stories and mythologies. When you arrive home after work (assuming you work outside the home), you cast off your work identity and adopt a different personal self. When you arrive at a party, you're a different person walking up to the door than after being welcomed inside. Your energy changes. Doorways define transitions, and we can use their magic to empower us on our paths.

Of course, not every home has a door in the middle of the front. That's okay. You can still enhance your doorway as a way to welcome energy, while treating the middle space at the front of your home as the area related to career and life path.

Love Your Door, Love Your Life

Within feng shui, the front door holds power as the mouth of chi, or good energy. Energy is attracted by front doors, and a great front door draws the eye through a combination of visual cues, contrasting materials, and functional objects. It leaves no doubt as to where the best place to enter the home is—which can be important if you have multiple or competing entrances. The front door should be clean, attractive, and free of any kind of debris or detritus.

I've worked with front doors—for my own family and with clients—for a long time, and I have observed how making changes to the front door allows for massive shifts in self-perception. The idea of attracting good energy makes sense to me, but even more so, I've noticed that how people feel about their front door seems to be directly connected with how they view their lives. A door that helps us make the transition between private and public spaces recognizes the major shift in mindset that accompanies us when we leave and enter our homes. Similarly, a front door that is attractive to other people or that is set up to attract a certain vibe of person will be more likely to bring more of that kind of energy into our lives. A door that sticks or that doesn't work usually belongs to a person who feels the same. Having a front door that we swoon over makes us love our life, period.

Creating a Great Transition Inside

The interior front entrance of a home is also a transitional space. Even if your home isn't blessed with a giant foyer, seek to carve out a welcoming moment upon entering. The goal isn't just to welcome guests—it's to welcome *you* in a way that helps you cast off whatever needs to be left outside. Style tips for a gorgeous front entry abound, but at the very least, consider incorporating the following:

CAREER & LIFE PATH

The mouth of energy, the front entrance, flow and good fortune

COLOR: *Black*

ELEMENT: *Water*

RELATED HOME ITEMS: *Fountain, mirror, sculpture with wavy lines, black doors, black house mats, shiny pots*

SHAPE: *Wavy lines or free-flowing organic forms*

- An overhead, interior light to illuminate the threshold.
- A hook for keys to ease coming and going.
- A greeting visual, like a piece of artwork, that captures exactly how you want to feel at home.
- A landing surface, like a small table or console. If you don't have room, install a wall shelf.
- A container or small tray where you can immediately place items.

Client Story: Work-at-Home Empowerment

Ginny is a work-from-home consultant who lives in a contemporary home tucked into a cul-de-sac, with the back facing a city forest. When I met with her, she was working from home and struggling over whether to accept a recent job offer.

The first thing we tackled was the path to her doorway. She had been quite busy, and the shrubs and pots along the path were either overgrown or dead. So she cleaned the doorway and entrance area and placed a larger rug.

Inside, Ginny's home has what is called a split view—where half the view is of a wall and the other half goes down a long hallway. When the eye doesn't know where to go, this can be a problem, so we placed a visual cue on the wall to guide the eye into the hallway. Essentially, this helped the energy move through the space.

Ginny's office was in a front room in the life path area of her energy map. Since her desk was facing a wall, I suggested she place it to face the room's entrance to help her feel more supported in her work. Ginny was feeling untethered as an at-home worker, and our creative solution was to frame some lanyards she had collected from attending work conferences.

The very next workday, out of the blue, Ginny received a completely different job offer and took it. She is still in that job today, and she now shares her office space with her husband, who also works at home.

Working on your front door energy has two great benefits: loving your home life even more and drawing positive energy into the home. If your door has any problems (it sticks, opens outward, can't be seen, and so on), fix them using the suggestions below. Your doorway is a rich metaphor for your life path, so use it regularly.

Consider your path: To draw the eye and good energy, ensure there's a meandering, well-lit path to the door.

Rest your feet: To ground the entrance, add a large, dark mat layered with a smaller mat, with or without welcoming language.

Announce the door: If your door is hard to notice, add a large-scale visual, like a sculpture or statement planter filled with a tall shrub or flowering plant.

Make the door attractive: Aim for a door that visually pops (because of its material or color), swings into the house, opens easily, locks perfectly, and isn't surrounded by clutter.

Use beautiful hardware: A door handle that feels substantial provides a sense of constancy and support.

Install gorgeous lighting: To attract good energy, make sure the entrance is well-lit, with either two sconces or one overhead light.

Choose stylish house numbers: Use house numbers in a font you adore, and place them in a straight horizontal line, which is considered more auspicious in feng shui.

FIND YOURSELF

How do you respond when you look at your front door?

Does the atmosphere in your front entrance allow you to cast off your previous self when you come inside?

15

HONOR WISDOM AND DEEPEN SELF-KNOWLEDGE

W e live in an information age that yearns for more wisdom. We might know which Harry Potter character we are most like, but not always how we can be the source of our own magic. We have entire worlds at our fingertips but so much to wade through that it becomes difficult to know who and what to trust, or even whether we can trust ourselves. When we're grappling with big questions of identity and personal growth, or wanting to enhance wisdom in general, the front left of our energy map should be the first place we investigate.

All of your rooms contain stories you are telling yourself about your life, but perhaps none more so than in this corner. Objects you place here, colors you use, the function of this space—all of these set the tone for your explorations of self in the rest of the home. Rather than think about the self you are reaching toward, I far prefer my clients to take an accurate assessment of what has shaped their life and to use this space as a reminder of what has been most important to them on their path to self-discovery. What lessons have you learned already? What lessons are you always relearning?

A Home for Insight

When you attend to this energy center of your space, you bring into alignment your views of yourself and the understanding you receive from the great mentors and thought leaders of your life. Enhance the area when you are building new skills, deepening your knowledge, looking for new insights, searching for the right teacher, or just seeking personal growth in any form.

When placed in this corner of your energy map, some types of rooms work beautifully, such as an office, the kitchen, the living room, or the main bedroom. Others are more difficult, such as a child's bedroom or the garage (see my story on page 164). But when this section of the home is fully dialed in energetically, expect ideas to flow easily, your sense of self to feel secure and confident, and your mind to be clear and quick. Overall, this is a good place in the home for displays of where you are on your educational path and for images of mentors and great influences. It is also a space in which to manifest self-love. It's a place where you can honor your needs for self-reflection, enforce healthy habits, and honor your personal truths.

In many modern suburban homes, the wisdom and self-knowledge area is often situated in the garage, which isn't in itself a problem. Garages don't necessarily have to be dark and dingy. Some of my clients have gone all-in on their garages, adding floor coatings to cover old stains, lights to improve illumination, and artwork of favorite people, like a tintype photo of Nick Offerman.

One client discovered she had lost her way on her own path, while her teenage daughter, who resided in their home's wisdom space, was a fully confident, self-actualized human. The client decided to work on the corner outside of the home, by adding a birdbath, to activate this energy for herself, since she didn't have complete control of her daughter's space.

This is also a great location to situate a personal library or to hang messages about what you know—about yourself and the world. Even a row of tools hung thoughtfully sends a powerful message about your ability to get things done. But what if you don't know who you are yet? Just as you can learn about yourself by trying on different styles of clothing in a store, you can discover who you are by playing with the objects, décor, and symbols in this space. Self-discovery doesn't have to be a high-stakes endeavor. It can also be fun.

WISDOM & SELF-KNOWLEDGE

The center of self-improvement, decision-making, skill sets, and education

COLORS: *Black, dark blue, green*

ELEMENTS: *Water and wood*

RELATED HOME ITEMS: *Fountain, mirror, shiny pots, wooden sculpture or furniture, books*

SHAPE: *Wavy lines or free-flowing organic forms*

CREATING A SPACE THAT
ENHANCES INSIGHT

Here are ways to enhance the energy in rooms related to wisdom and self-knowledge:

- Keep this area clean and uncluttered.

- Add objects that represent what you want to learn or improve upon.

- Display books or posters that symbolize what you'd like to learn or have learned.

- Bring in water elements like a fountain or an image of water.

- Exhibit images of thought leaders, creators, or mentors you admire, such as using a bust (which I love).

- Think black or dark blue for objects or décor.

- Reinforce ideas that support your understanding of self with images of self-love.

- Install adequate lighting, especially lamps with bare, visible bulbs.

- Install a mirror to increase your ability to self-reflect.

Making Space for Forgiveness

My husband, Adam, had been hounding me for months about helping him clean out our garage, which meant going through the boxes of personal mementos I had carted across the world for the past twenty years. I had a massive block with it. Honestly, I was afraid to be reminded of the person I had been in my twenties—someone who left a trail of broken relationships in three countries. There would be letters. There would be a reckoning. Needless to say, I put it off as long as I could.

My ancestral family never could figure out how to think about garages. We always packed them until they were full, just throwing things inside like they were great dumping grounds for psychic denial. When I discovered that our home's wisdom and self-knowledge energy center resided entirely in our overflowing garage, I was less than thrilled. It took weeks to work up the courage to confront my old self and deal with the mess.

When I did, I found some real gems, of course. A poem I wrote about my shame for loving *NSYNC. A letter I wrote to a friend I don't even remember being in love with. A full-size self-portrait nude that a guy once sent me. A copy of my parents' divorce decree.

As I went through everything, I had so much compassion for that young human who was trying to figure out how to be in the world (and by the way, I now unapologetically love *NSYNC). I found that I was able to forgive my past self wholly and just throw out anything that made me feel shame. I felt remade in the process.

FIND YOURSELF

What part of yourself do you want to grow?
What could you put in this area to support that desire?

16

CELEBRATE FAMILY
AND LINEAGE

amilies are complicated, beautiful, exasperating, sublime, fascinating, and maddening. They are constant and ever-evolving. They can be the source of our greatest joys and our deepest hurts. They provide an outlet for our trenchant desire to love and our greatest lessons in how to accept other people. The way we feel about our families influences whether we make spatial choices to love, honor, or even just acknowledge them.

As you attend to this area of your home's energy map, consider who you see as your family, how you want to support those relationships in your life, and what would increase feelings of security and stability. I suggest thinking expansively about the concept of family: It can be a combination of your biological family and your "chosen" family, or all those friends and mentors who are as close as family. Also, work on this section of the home when you are starting a new project, since it is associated with the excitement of new beginnings.

Honoring Family

I love how people tell the stories of their family in their spaces. Some families plaster their walls with images of each other. Others are less obvious, preferring to display symbolic objects, like a vase inherited from a favorite aunt, whose meaning is private. When people keep pictures of their families on glassed-in bookshelves, I find that usually indicates relationships that need to be healed. Others maintain their connection to loved ones who've died through elaborate altars.

If you find yourself feeling alone, surround yourself with symbols of your chosen family—whoever they may be—which can help you feel supported by community. Get creative and choose whatever makes sense for your space. A corkboard covered with photos of your lifelong besties works just as well as family portraiture.

Further, we can honor whatever we want in relation to our families while discarding what we no longer identify with. I like to think of this as our inheritance. At some point, we get to decide what parts of our past we embrace as part of our own value system. The rest we can discard. The family center is a great location for any imagery or relics connecting to your ancestral past, to important people from your lineage, and to your ethnic background and identity.

Finally, if people who live together are not getting along, adding some visual cues can strengthen the relationships. If children are squabbling, for example, place a happy picture of just those children somewhere in the family area. This practice is more subtle but no less effective than the other tactic I've used with my own kids: making them both put on one of their father's gigantic shirts at the same time.

Energetic Enhancements

In the world of feng shui, the family and ancestors are connected most strongly to the wood and water elements. Enhancements made with wood should be helpful in activating this center. Consider adding some of the following to strengthen your family ties or create new ones:

- Add living, vigorous plants, especially jade.

- Add long, columnar shapes, reaching vertical from floor to ceiling, in the form of columns, drapes, or wooden floor lamps.

- Place objects you associate with existing family members or ancestors.

- Add flowers in a glass vase.

- Incorporate an object that symbolizes a new project you want to take on.

FAMILY & ANCESTORS

The location for ancestors, family, and new beginnings

COLORS: *Green, blue*

ELEMENTS: *Wood and water*

RELATED HOME ITEMS: *Plants, wooden figures, wooden sculptures, mirrors, fountains, aquariums, flowers in vases, family portraits*

SHAPE: *Columns or strong verticals*

PRACTICING FORGIVENESS

I have a spatial process I often use when I am struggling to forgive someone, and I recommend it to anyone who has been hurt by someone they trusted or loved. Only do this when you feel ready to forgive. How do you know when that is? To me, it's when the yearning to feel unburdened of old hurts allows us to let go of the desire for a different outcome. We long for a feeling of lightness. If that describes what you desire, try this practice, which can help you move toward forgiveness.

- In a prominent place, like the fridge, place an image of the person from a time when you had a good relationship.

- Every time you pass the image, say to yourself: *I forgive you, you forgive me.*

- Notice as forgiveness grows within you. When the image no longer causes hurt or dark feelings, but leaves you with the warmth of possibility, you're ready to take it down.

Note: This process is not meant to replace therapy, especially if trauma relates to abuse or violence. At first, you can expect some feelings of discomfort when doing this, but if you find the image is triggering, by all means abandon the practice.

Client Story: Allowing Boundaries to Blossom

My client Kylie couldn't figure out how to maintain a loving relationship with her family of origin. She had grown up in a Christian fundamentalist household but had expanded her ideas of what life could look like when she married and built her own family. Even though she and her husband both worked in a church themselves, the widening gulf she felt with her family was stressing her out.

Kylie had just purchased a new home, and a row of gorgeous roses was planted right outside the family and lineage area of her energy map. To me, roses are a rich and potent symbol for engaging with family— wait for the blooms, but beware the thorns. Has there ever been a plant humans love that is so clearly a lesson in personal boundaries?

In her house, Kylie also wasn't displaying any pictures of her extended family of origin, which was telling. I suggested she find and put up a photo that captured a time when she was most attached to the people she grew up with. That way, she could always remember the positive base for her family relationship.

Kylie's family might never stop wanting her to be someone else, but Kylie could set healthy boundaries and focus on the parts of their shared history she appreciated. This would help her engage with them on her own terms. Though they had lived hours apart for several years, she soon found herself on a house hunt with them as they looked for a place in her hometown. She felt ready for it.

FIND YOURSELF

What old hurts are you holding on to?
Are you ready to let them go?

Who do you consider to be part of your family?
How might you honor them in your space?

17

DEFINE WEALTH
AND BUILD PROSPERITY

n my home, an entire corner of the living room is devoted to symbols of wealth and prosperity, though others might not realize it. On our open shelves, there's a painting of Grosvenor Square in London (my *very* distant ancestors were wealthy landowners), a giant piece of driftwood, an antique Cadillac headlight, a jade tree, a green glass bowl filled with coins, a large piece of quartz, and a basket of cat toys. These objects may seem purely decorative, but they tell my family story of wealth and prosperous growth (okay, maybe not the cat toys).

Everyone defines wealth in their own ways. For some, wealth is strictly measured by money, while others believe money is the least-important resource. Some feel wealthy when they have "enough," by whatever standard, to meet their needs, while others don't feel comfortable unless they have a giant nest egg saved for a rainy day. For some, money flows freely into, and sometimes out of, their lives, while others consider money a limiting, necessary evil. Typically, our attitudes toward wealth are formed by our experiences of scarcity and abundance as children.

As a result, how we address this area of our home's energy map will reflect our personal history and ideas about wealth. In fact, I prefer to use the term *prosperity* rather than *wealth*. Prosperity is a more universal concept that includes all aspects of abundance, growth, and hope.

In classic feng shui, the energy center for wealth and prosperity sits in the northwest corner of the energy map. This is an excellent place in the home to tell your story of wealth by using the art of placement with both classic symbols of wealth and prosperity and personal objects that embody wealth to you. The goal is to tell your personal story about where you'd like to be on your path toward prosperity.

Prosperous Enhancements

As I say, anything that embodies wealth can work, but common objects include plants, hardware, and crystals. Anything made with wood is a fitting energy enhancement for this area, as is flowing water in the form of a small table fountain, images of water, or mirrors, which are considered to be of the water element in feng shui.

PLANTS AND WOOD

Anything considered wood is a classic feng shui adjustment for wealth and prosperity, as are houseplants, which tell a story of continued prosperity and growth (as long as they are in good health).

Here are some plants that are considered lucky:

- Money tree
- Jade
- Rubber plant
- Snake plant
- Eucalyptus
- Bamboo
- Ficus ginseng
- Citrus trees
- Arrowhead plant

HARDWARE

It's said that hardware is "the jewelry of the home." So if you want a quick fix to foster a more prosperous home, upgrade the hardware on furniture, cabinets, light switches, or light fixtures anywhere in the house, but especially within this part of the energy map. This can do wonders to send a powerful message of wealth without busting budgets. Design maxims hold that you should pick two hardware finishes that go together and use them throughout the house, but it doesn't all have to match.

PERSONAL WEALTH OBJECTS

It seems ironic to spend money in order to signal wealth and prosperity. Instead, find an object you already own that

WEALTH & PROSPERITY

The site of money, growth, hope, and abundance

COLORS: *Purple, green, blue, metallic*

ELEMENT: *Wood*

RELATED HOME ITEMS: *Plants, wood furniture, crystals, wood sculptures and figures, images of water, moving water*

SHAPE: *Columns*

represents wealth to you, whether it is of high monetary value or only personal, emotional value. This might include a cherished heirloom, an expensive clock, a vintage camera—whatever says, "I am wealthy and prosperous." For me, it's a Lalique cat sculpture my grandfather once bought for my grandmother during a trip to Europe. We don't have too many stories of extravagance in our family, but this one recalls a time when my grandfather happily supported something his wife desired in the moment. This cat has traveled the world to get to me—and that feels like wealth. What could it be for you?

THE MEANINGS OF CRYSTALS

Amethyst
Ideation and prosperity

Alexandrite
Manifestation

Garnet
Dreams and insight

Jade
Vision

Citrine
Wealth maintenance

Green Aventurine
Creativity and pioneering spirit

Celestine
Bliss

Smoky Quartz
Removal of blockages

Clear Quartz
Goal-setting

CRYSTALS

The word *crystal* comes from the Greek word for "ice," as the ancient Greeks believed that crystals were made of water frozen so completely they became solid. Like many ancient people, the Greeks used natural crystals to fortify their spirits and their health, sometimes grinding them into a powder they would rub all over their bodies. Did it work? Does it matter?

Crystals are gorgeous decorative additions to nearly any home and come in every color. They are earth energy in its most pristine, visually stunning form, and the mere sight of them can feel more grounding. Of course, not everyone wants to live with a shelf of craggy quartz (I do!), but I counsel clients to invest in high-quality, single crystals to add to their wealth corners.

WATER

Anything connected to the element of water works in the wealth and prosperity corner. Fountains and aquariums are great, but if those aren't your thing, consider mirrors or even images of water. Remember, symbolic additions work just as well as literal ones to cue your story of wealth and prosperity. Also, whenever you place an item in your wealth corner, express gratitude for your continued prosperity.

Client Story: Creating a Free Flow of Wealth

My client Grace always felt like everything in her very busy family life was "up in the air," especially her family's finances. Money came in, money flew out. She wanted a new role in her company, with higher compensation, greater visibility, and more responsibility, but she felt overwhelmed by the potential change and all of the loose ends at home.

The first thing I noticed was that Grace entered her home through the back door, which was located in the wealth and prosperity energy center. The front door barely got used.

Lots of people enter their homes through doors other than the front door. If that is the case for you, switching your habits and using the front door could open your home to new ideas and energies. But if that is not possible, make sure you always love coming home. If you enter through a utility room, garage, or side door, make that experience a beautiful one. This will help you honor the transition between your life outside the home and the energies brewing at home.

In Grace's case, she entered through their laundry room, where the stacked washing machine and dryer were literally tossing water up in the air. Thus, it made sense that she felt financially tossed about—since she had a reminder every time she walked in the door.

Grace made some minor adjustments to her laundry room, including adding a citrine crystal on top of the washer/dryer. Within a week, she got the promotion, and she started to feel far more at ease in her family's financial life.

FIND YOURSELF

How would you describe your current mindset around accumulating and attracting wealth?

What are some immediate adjustments you could make to your space in order to signal to yourself that you are living a wealthy and prosperous life?

18

GAIN INFLUENCE IN YOUR COMMUNITIES

W anting to be liked—it's the scourge of the social animal, isn't it? Not all of us need to be the most beloved personality who walks the earth, but we do want to be seen, heard, appreciated, and acknowledged in the settings that matter. These are basic desires and healthy human aspirations. In feng shui, this is traditionally called the fame and reputation energy center, but I prefer calling it our center of influence. That puts the power back in our own hands.

Fame, reputation, recognition, leadership, status—these qualities all come back to how confident we feel shining our own inner light and where we want that light to be directed. If you are ready to raise your voice, be seen as a leader or a valued contributor, get attention for your contributions, or overall gain influence, then the area of the home associated with fire energy is calling to you.

When you enhance this area, you can expect to feel more passionate about whatever it is you are doing and more respected by your colleagues, peers, friends, and customers (if you have them). You will feel more inspired about the aspects of life you care about. The influence center is all about getting noticed, freeing yourself up to shine, and receiving credit for all of the hard work you are doing.

Even if you don't think of yourself as a born leader, you can certainly cultivate the right level of influence for you. It's just a matter of looking for the places where you would like your voice to be heard. When choosing how to decorate and enhance this area, consider the wide range of community settings where you have impact, which may include your relationships within the home, with colleagues at your workplace, with clients (if you're in business), with your spiritual community, with social groups like book clubs, with community or advocacy groups, and even within digital communities.

Shine Your Light

Here are some ways you can embody your own shiny, bright self in this area of the home:

- Hang wallpaper that perfectly encapsulates how you want to be perceived. Consider animal imagery, bold colors (to be seen as bold), striking patterns, symbolic plants, and other personalized images.
- Display certificates, accolades, trophies, and plaques.
- Use design elements that guide the attention upward, like lighting, triangle patterns, and floor lamps.
- Exhibit images of yourself doing your thing, and in the settings where you want to have an impact.
- Install plants, especially spiky plants like cacti (but avoid them in other parts of the home).
- Decorate with objects you associate with your personal success.

Client Story: Teaching People How to See You

Dennis lived in a house where his main bathroom was located in the fame and reputation area. It was at the end of a long hallway, and he could see the bathroom when he opened the front door. This had a couple of potential effects on his life. For one, he wanted to be better recognized in his field, but he was struggling with relationships with his colleagues. He also wanted to improve some of his friend relationships, as he had recently been dealing with a breakdown of boundaries. Symbolically, it is a problem if your reputation is in the toilet.

INFLUENCE, OR FAME & REPUTATION

The locus of fame, reputation, recognition, and leadership

COLORS: *Red, orange*

ELEMENT: *Fire*

RELATED HOME ITEMS: *Candles, lighting, fireplaces, electronics, animals*

SHAPE: *Triangle, pointed shapes*

Bathrooms in the home can be an energy issue wherever they reside, but especially in this location, so our first goal was to remove the view of the space from the front door. Dennis added a Japanese half-curtain called a noren to the hallway, blocking the view from the doorway. In the bathroom, he added better organization, as well as a candle to add fire energy. Rather than store products on counters, he added shelving with some objects positioned solely for their attractiveness.

Dennis experienced a giant shift with these changes, including a complete breakup with his toxic friend circle and finding a publisher for a book he was working on. While he had worked on other areas of his home, addressing this part of his home shaped his life in a big way.

KEEP PEOPLE AT YOUR TABLE LONGER

Invite people to your physical table and keep them there by creating a serene and focused eating environment. To get people to slow down and really share the moment, add these fixes:

- Choose a round table, which tends to have no preferable spots.

- Place people whose attention wanders with their backs to the kitchen.

- Use chairs with cushions and enclosed arms to keep guests contained and supported.

- Light a candle in the center of the table or use an eye-catching centerpiece.

- Serve food family-style in passable serving dishes so everyone has to engage.

- Define the space with a pendant light; during dinner, turn this on and the others off.

FIND YOURSELF

What exactly would you like to be known for?

What's a simple gathering you could put together within the next month—one that will allow for an exchange of ideas with people you enjoy?

19

SHARE LOVE AND STRENGTHEN PARTNERSHIPS

reating a balance between partners in a modern home is one of life's most interesting and meaningful design challenges— and how could it not be so? Just consider how much gender roles have changed in society and the massive personal reconfiguration that forming a partnership requires.

Ultimately, however, gender and sexual preferences don't matter, nor do community attitudes toward traditional gender roles. The only thing that truly matters is the personal dynamic between the partners themselves and how they use the power of home design to support and express their relationship. Typically, the task of shaping the home falls to the person who cares the most or has the most power in the relationship. The key is to keep a light heart and shared love at the forefront throughout the process.

When you work on the love and marriage energy center of your home, you can invite new vigor into an existing relationship or manifest a new love relationship entirely. Often, this entails a considered and careful rethinking of a couple's goals for companionship or a single person's desire for a relationship. Further, since love tends to radiate, anything you change here tends to extend throughout the home.

Partnerships Are a Magical Mix

Homes built by partners can feel like they have their style dialed in because there is magic in the mixing of two persuasions. In fact, in recent years, many compelling and popular styles illustrate the synergy that occurs when two different ideas rub up against each other. Consider modern farmhouse, Japandi, modern bohemian, Memphis deco, grandmillennial, and cottagecore. On the surface, two ideas can often seem at odds. Together, they can become more than the sum of their parts.

Couples thrive when they are curious about each partner's taste and explore the world of decoration together. Often, designers will choose an overall theme or palette for a home and will then let one part of the couple take over the smaller choices within different spaces so that they can see their own visions realized. That seems to work well for some couples, since it gives partners one little area of the world that is an embodiment of their own vision. For larger spaces, it makes more sense to have both partners involved in the decision-making and to make choices with all family members in mind.

Here are some other things to keep in mind as you explore how your partnership can find expression within your home. The following ideas can apply to the specific area of interest on your energy map, or to the rooms where love and relationships are best fostered. So if you want to strengthen a partnership, you can employ cues for partnership in the love and partnership area, throughout the home, or in the bedroom.

SEEK SYMMETRY

Humans love symmetry. Some posit that it is a way for the eye to find order in an unpredictable world, a moment of calm amid visual chaos. In feng shui, symmetry represents equality in partnership. Use this maxim to create a visual metaphor of equality in any space. You don't need to put doubles everywhere, but artfully placed pairs add balance and tell a story. Think about adding the following:

LOVE & PARTNERSHIP

The center of love, marriage, and sex

COLORS: *Brown, yellow, pink, peach*

ELEMENT: *Earth*

RELATED HOME ITEMS: *Ceramics, tile, terra-cotta planters, clay figures or sculpture, crystals*

SHAPE: *Square or rectangle*

- Paired sets of bookshelves
- Two matching chairs or matching sofas facing each other
- Sets of two framed and related prints or artworks
- Sets of two bookends
- Two candlesticks
- Pairs of figurines
- Imagery of couples or two similar items grouped together

TERRITORIALITY

If you and your partner long to remain tigers in the sack, you might consider being like tigers in the rest of the home, too. People have territorial tendencies, so carving out spaces that belong to one partner alone can help them feel empowered. Partnership suffers greatly in homes where one partner has not a single square foot of space that is entirely their own.

TEMPERATURE

It's a surprise to no one, but everyone has their own ideal room temperature, and conflicts over temperature are common. Environmental psychologists say people tend to get along better in warmer climes, but not too warm. About 70 degrees Fahrenheit is the ideal, since most bodily functions work best at this temperature. Maybe this makes for a silly home date night, but consider dedicating an evening to finding your ideal home temperature.

Bedroom Considerations

Of course, wherever it's located on your home's energy map, the bedroom is a key space in any partnership. While much recent media attention has focused on simple adjustments for getting a full night's rest, few experts have laid out best practices for how to arrange the bedroom thoughtfully for partnership.

SHARED VIEWS

Within the bedroom, one design constellation can have detrimental consequences for a partnership, and that is the view from the bed. If a couple has a split view—say, one partner looks through a door and down a hallway, and the other gazes at a dresser—this can foster separate visions for their lives. If possible, position the bed so that its view isn't cut in half. If that can't be done, keep the door closed and create a dominant visual on the other half that will draw the eye.

DIFFICULT CONVERSATIONS

When partners need to have a hard talk, they should consider a space other than the bed or the bedroom. First, it can often feel less tense when you can sit side by side, depending on how you respond to looking into someone else's eyes. As an added bonus, you won't create a lingering atmosphere of conflict and anger in the bedroom after the conversation is over.

SEXUALITY

Partners can heighten sexual response without outfitting their bedroom like a Las Vegas love palace. The key is to include thoughtful but personal details that remind both partners that they are sexual beings. Focus on touch—touchable fabrics, sumptuous pillows, a carpeted floor underneath. Or use visual cues that have personal meaning but aren't necessarily overtly sexual. This might be the place for a new tiger figurine, but any inside joke works. In our bedroom, the best sign of all is the way the doorknob looks when it's locked. I can text a picture of a locked door to my partner, and it's better than more obvious choices.

Singles: Manifesting a Relationship

If you are unpartnered but wish to change that, consider adding some of the ideas in the preceding sections. Many times I have visited the home of a single person who longs to be tethered to someone else, and their bed is set up for a single person, with only one end table and lamp, or the bed is pushed up against the wall so no person could come join them. As you visualize your ideal partner, make room for that person in your space right now. By doing so, you are telling yourself the story that you are open and ready for that special person coming your way.

FOSTER RITUAL TOGETHERNESS

Can't always carve out time for date night? You can still design your home in ways that foster ritual togetherness and prioritize your partnership. This is important for long-term couples; one study found that partners who had regular couple rituals were more satisfied with their relationships than those who didn't.[23]

The key is to choose an activity that's easy to re-create, and designate a space for that purpose. Here are some possibilities:

- A couch or loveseat for Netflix and chill

- A bench in a lovely spot of the yard for watching the birds

- A porch swing for a weekly cocktail hour

- A double hammock in which to slow down and snuggle together

- A double-headed shower

- A two-person sauna

- A bistro table and chairs for a balcony or small terrace

Client Story: Attracting Love to a Busy Life

Tanya had just moved cross-country to Seattle, the city she grew up in. She was finding it difficult to meet new people for romance and was worried that her commitment to her new job was getting in the way of her life. She had purchased a one-bedroom condo and had her own style and comfort completely dialed in.

However, Tanya's work-from-home desk was situated exactly in the love and relationship corner of her condo, along with plaques and accolades from her professional life. Where the energies of love, sexuality, and partnership might be, she had created a corporate setting. Honestly, if you love your job, having a work desk in this area isn't a terrible idea, since it also connects to self-love. But Tanya was seeking partnership, so this setup was less than beneficial.

Together, Tanya and I moved the desk and rethought her bedroom, which was a classic single person's setup. She was reticent to change it, but with some new cues of coupledom added to her work desk, she found herself with a regular influx of new dates. Within half a year, she was in a long-term partnership.

FIND YOURSELF

Has one person in your partnership made most of the design decisions in your home? How might the other partner's needs and desires be brought into the story through design?

Do you desire partnership where there is none? List the ways that you might make space for partnership in your home.

20

INVITE CREATIVITY AND
THE ENERGY OF CHILDREN

have a dedicated art studio with a ceramics wheel, a corner with an easel lit by the sun through a skylight, a perfect hand-carved desk in a room filled with floor-to-ceiling bookshelves, and a perfect chair dedicated to my morning reading—all laid out in the dream home of my imagination. That I actually own none of these things (yet) doesn't mean that I don't live in a house of wild, free-flowing, exuberant creativity. After all, we have a decent kitchen table just like everybody else.

Creativity is every human's birthright. We are all creative, even if we don't work in a creative industry or have beautiful spaces devoted to making art. If you don't identify as creative, chances are good that you just haven't found your medium yet, or you haven't defined a space in your home and your life for creativity.

When you work on this section of your energy map, you can expect more joy in general, a lighthearted, childlike spirit, more creative inspiration, and good vibes. It can help launch any new creative adventure. Since this area is also connected to the spirit of children, look closely at this space when you are trying to add to your family or when the children in your life need extra support. Most of this chapter's advice fosters creativity in any space, but it has added impact in this section of the home.

Designing Space for Creativity

When you designate a specific space in your home to creative practice, your mind becomes primed toward creativity every time you enter that space. It doesn't need to be a room; a desk, a workbench, or even a comfy chair can suffice. Naming these places is the first step toward making creativity a part of your life.

However, each year also brings emerging insights into the environmental adjustments that help human ingenuity thrive. Designing your own space in itself can even increase productivity. Researchers at the University of Edinburgh have shown that this can increase productivity by up to 32 percent.[24]

Here are some other design elements that inspire creativity:

The color blue: To think outside of the box, look at something blue. Gazing at shades of blue makes people more likely to exhibit divergent thinking (red does the opposite).[25]

Fire: Fires are pleasurable. They reduce blood pressure and get us in a dreamy frame of mind.[26] This works whether the fire is real or a video image, a full fireplace, or a candle.

Curves: People respond more positively and become more relaxed in spaces with prominent curved lines and forms, whether in the form of curved furniture or curved walls.[27] Curves always help to move energy.

Art: Looking at art ignites our creativity and resets the mind in the same way that looking at nature does. In fact, studies show this causes a 10 percent increase in blood to the brain.[28]

High ceilings: No wonder so many artists live in lofts. People who work in rooms with ten-foot ceilings (or higher) have been shown to score better on tests of creativity than those in less tall spaces.[29]

Energy Enhancements for Creativity

As the center for children and creativity, this space does well with enhancements connected to those themes. Try working these things into this space:

- The color yellow in whatever incarnation you like (from cream to sunshine)
- Objects made out of earthenware
- Children's artwork, games, and toys
- Photos of children
- Games, art materials, and artworks that speak to the creative process
- Musical instruments
- Square shapes

Client Story: Tapping into Creative Flow

Sometimes, a few energetic shifts to a space can make all the difference. My client Kim had gone to school for art, but after having kids and working a series of office jobs, she had not picked up a paintbrush in years. She wanted to make more space in their historic 1940s cottage not just for her own creative life but for her children, who showed signs of budding artistry.

Their home's children and creativity energy center spanned several spaces—part of the main bedroom, a closet, the living room, and part of the garage. Unfortunately, their cat of twenty years, who was dying, also used part of this space; his litter box was in the closet. Our first task was to figure out a new arrangement for the kitty that wasn't disorienting for her.

Kim also decided to move her old artwork into this closet and to fix its light. She looked through her old canvases and creations from twenty years prior, reorganized the closet, and got rid of any art that she didn't absolutely love.

As the weeks passed, she started hanging out more with a colleague to sing. Eventually, they formed a band and started performing. Kim is much happier now that she has made space for her creative life, even though she couldn't have predicted the form that creativity would take.

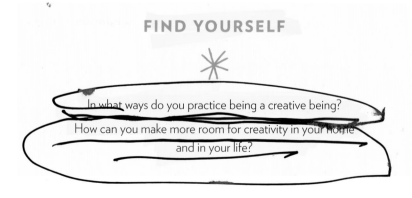

FIND YOURSELF

In what ways do you practice being a creative being? How can you make more room for creativity in your home and in your life?

21

WELCOME HELPFUL PEOPLE
AND MAKE ROOM FOR TRAVEL

No one does it alone—even if sometimes we feel like we are the only person we can count on. We need support, help, and guidance as we seek to accomplish something meaningful and useful with others and in the world.

All sections of the energy map connect to the world outside our home's walls, but none as explicitly as the travel and helpful people area. Focus on this space if you're ready for a new mentor, you want the existing people in your life to play a bigger role, you long for guidance (including from spirits from the past), you just generally need support, or you want more travel in your life.

Why do the energies of travel and helpful people occupy the same space? Travel doesn't have to be about consumption. It could involve bringing your own perspective to the place you visit. And receiving help doesn't have to be about consumption. You help others by receiving from them graciously. In this way, traveling and being of service both involve a reciprocal exchange of good energy.

Movement Attracts Change and Good Energy

In general, the outside areas in front of the home are particularly responsive to any physical and metaphorical winds and changing energy. This applies to all types of change, and not just to change associated with this area of the energy map. To attract good energy into the home, consider adding some kind of wind-capturing device, which transforms unruly breezes into something beautiful. Classic feng shui enhancements include wind socks, kinetic sculptures, and wind chimes.

Chimes are the absolute best way to transform negative energy into positive energy coming into the home. They're a classic good luck enhancement to any environment, and they work by slowing down and redistributing energy. But don't overdo it. More chimes does not create more good vibes, and homes with thirty sets of chimes out front make me worry for the homeowner. Instead, choose only one or two, and test them in person so you know you like the sound. Consider your own tonal preferences and cultural attachments. The best tend to be metal chimes, those with hollow metal cylinders; smaller chimes are brighter, while larger chimes are more resonant. Some chimes are tuned to evoke famous compositions (like "Ode to Joy"), while others evoke specific places (like Kyoto, Provence, or Bavaria).

Good places to hang chimes include by the front door or entrance, in the front corner by the travel and helpful people area, or just outside of the creativity center.

Kinetic sculptures are another good choice, and some people prefer them since they are silent. Metal sculptures grounded in the earth that move with the wind create a strong visual embodiment of responsiveness to flow. Sometimes called wind spinners or wind catchers, these poetic metaphors can enhance this center and get things moving in your life.

Manifesting Travel

If you yearn for travel but your life doesn't have room for it, determine whether the spatial makeup of your home lacks this area entirely. I often find a relationship between a missing travel corner and a lack of time or space for adventure. If that's the case, create a corner in your yard by planting a tree, placing a rock, burying a crystal, installing a light, or filling in lush landscaping where that corner would be.

If you have already experienced travel, whether to far-flung places or beloved locales closer to home, bring images, souvenirs, and objects from your wanderings into this space to enhance your relationship to travel. What's your dream trip? What would it take to get you there? Don't send yourself the message, "I have always wanted to go to Tahiti." Embody the message, "I am going to Tahiti." Here are objects you could place in this space:

- A postcard (or a poster) from your desired destination
- Objects from your travels
- A travel mood board collecting the experiences you want to have
- Current travel guides for ideal destinations
- A picture of the person you want to travel with

Call in Guidance

If you are looking for help or need more support and guidance, focus on this area of the energy map. Put out a call for whoever fits your needs, be they mentors, teachers, wise elders, spiritual guides, work colleagues, therapists, or just friendly companions. One effective approach is to create an altar, one that embodies the type of help you are looking for. This altar could include these things:

- Tokens or gifts you've received from guides
- Images of your guides
- Personal notes of affirmation from helpful people
- Spiritual symbols or objects

Another idea is to imagine your own personal board of directors to help you run your life. Who are the people that you'd pull together? Imagine them all sitting at the same table, with you there as the chairperson and CEO. Draw a seating plan for your ideal board members and hide it in this area of the home.

Seek to Be of Service

You can use this area of the home to focus on how you, too, can be a person of service. Don't just ask for help, offer help, whether that's to better serve your household, your community, the earth and its creatures, your clients, your coworkers, and so on. On an altar or in a display, perhaps add something from the following list.

- Language or phrases that get you motivated and purposeful
- Images that remind you of the recipients of your service
- Books or posters that keep you motivated and on task

Client Story: Create an Inviting Space

When I worked with Claire and her husband Kai, they had recently moved to a new community for a better lifestyle, but almost a year later, they hadn't really met their people yet. Kai was traveling all the time, and Claire was trying to find a balance between managing the children's lives and her own. They had frequent discussions about how to arrange the new house in ways that met Kai's need for minimalism and Claire's need for an evocative home life. They loved their new house—except for a giant room in the front right, which had huge, twenty-foot ceilings and took up everything but the entrance. Claire had thought it would be a cozy hangout space in which to connect, but only their black lab wanted to be there. Kai wanted it to be his music studio.

Can one space do multiple things? Yes, but for this couple, it meant rethinking their generic living room. I suspected that the nothingness they felt in this space reflected their lack of connection to their community and their amorphous work/life boundaries.

I was confident that defining the space could help the couple integrate. They settled on the new idea of a creativity den. They acquired a giant rug to define the space as separate from the entrance and dialed in a shared style called *Boho-navian*, a nod to bohemian vibes paired with classic midcentury Scandinavian design. This, more than anything else, got them on the same page and helped them feel at home in their new place.

They acquired two upholstered chairs without arms—perfect for jamming on the guitar with a friend. They hung a modern metal mobile to add interest in the cavernous space above their heads. And they painted the walls a deep navy, which made it feel more den-like and cozy. Within a week, a close musician friend contacted them to visit (and jam) after a long absence. Claire decided to cut back her hours to be more helpful to her immediate family, and as this area filled with activity, Kai looked for other job opportunities that wouldn't require as much travel.

FIND YOURSELF

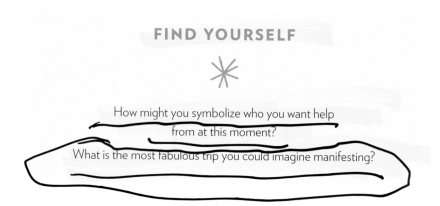

How might you symbolize who you want help from at this moment?

What is the most fabulous trip you could imagine manifesting?

22

ENHANCE SPIRITUALITY
AND WELL-BEING

never expected to become a churchgoer. Despite growing up in one of the most religiously ordered places in America, I had always been uncomfortable with any public displays of private belief, and I would have balked at sharing that on my walls in a space where we welcome guests. So no one was more surprised than me when I found myself looking for ways to add a connection to spirituality at the center of our home in order to remind myself of my emerging faith consciousness. Only now do I fully understand that homes are for shaping the self, not presenting a self to the world.

At the same time that I was exploring spiritual communities in my hometown, I began working with the center of our home, where our stairs, front hall, and opening space converge. I pulled out a contemporary artist's sculptural rendering of a cross we had received as a wedding present. I hung a Victorian punchwork with Christian themes that had been a source of great curiosity when it resided in my grandparents' home. I visited a local monastery where a monk had created house blessings that looked like the page of a medieval manuscript. My husband and I went shopping for a carpet for our front hall.

Giving a physical representation to my budding spirituality helped me move forward in the process. In the summer of my fortieth year, I got baptized—complete with a public dunk in a flowy, shapeless gown.

The Center Relates to Everything in the Home

The center of the home isn't necessarily a place we think about much. It can be part of a room, or a walk-through space, or the bottom of the stairs. Sometimes access to it is blocked entirely. But metaphorically, the space around the exact geographical center corresponds to our sense of health, our spirituality, and our overall well-being. So as you make adjustments in other areas, also take a good look at what is going on there. When this area of the home is well tended to, you should expect great vitality, fewer illnesses and physical injuries, emotional stability, and an overall positive flow of good things in your life. It's kind of the hub of the wheel that keeps everything else turning.

It can be a problem if a home doesn't provide good access to the center. Ideally, energy flows freely through the front door and circulates throughout the house, but if it can't actually reach the center, a home's inhabitants may experience a downturn in overall well-being. Or a long hallway or staircase can send the energy careening out of the picture. In those cases, the best approach is always to add elements that allow energy to circulate in the center of the home. You can easily determine where your house energy is flowing when you open your front door— just follow where your eye naturally goes. If that area is cluttered—stop me if you've heard this before—unclutter it immediately.

Make a Centering Moment

Too often, we connect our spaces purely to their function, leaving no place where we can think about questions of spirituality, overall well-being, and our nonmaterial aspirations. Whether you have a defined spiritual practice or not, this is where you can create robust imagery for the kind of balance and emotional backdrop you want to pervade everything else.

SPIRITUALITY & WELL-BEING

The center of the home, integration, harmony, and vitality

COLORS: *Yellow, earth tones*

ELEMENT: *Earth*

RELATED HOME ITEMS: *Ceramics, terra-cotta, dirt (with plants), brick, concrete, figures, pots, square frames, crystals*

SHAPE: *Square*

- Display any religious or spiritual symbology.
- Add something physically heavy for metaphorical groundedness and gravitas.
- Hang a house blessing that has meaning for you and your family (see page 204).
- Frame a favorite saying, family motto, or principle, and display it prominently so all can see it.
- Hang photos or portraits of people who ground you.
- Create an altar, such as on a small table, or a tableaux that collects the objects and symbols you find emblematic of well-being.
- Bring light to this area in the form of sconces, pendants, or a lamp on a small table.

WRITE A HOUSE BLESSING

The center of the home welcomes all of your big-picture benedictions for your household. Write a house blessing after doing a space clearing, at the start of the New Year, or whenever you move into a new space. It need not be denominational; feel free to use whatever language fits your spiritual practice. Many traditions have their own specific blessings, and the process here is meant to accommodate a variety of traditions.

1. Gather your materials and create a small altar at the center of the home. All you need is a surface, a piece of beautiful fabric, a beautiful rock or crystal, and a candle.

2. Light the candle and imagine the life you want for the home's occupants.

3. Write your blessing on a piece of paper. Here are some sample prompts you might use:

    May this home be filled with _____.
    May [your spiritual deity] watch over this home and imbue it with

    _____.

    Protect me/us from _____.
    Remind us that_____.
    I/We thank you for _____.

4. Place the house blessing on the surface and put the rock or crystal on top of it. Let the candle burn for an hour.

Enhancements for Personal Health

When our overall health declines, our feelings can be dominated by malaise, or we can be overcome with anxiety and other imbalances. While spatial design is never a direct fix for a health problem, making adjustments in the center of the home often leads to an overall increase in well-being that can have a profound effect on our state of health. Try these suggestions:

- Display any important art that reminds you of vitality and health.
- Add plants, like golden pothos, snake plant, cast-iron plant, or other low-light options.
- Hang images that embody vitality to you, like lush landscapes.
- Place a small desk fountain on a table to create circulating energy.
- Hang a faceted crystal nine, eighteen, or twenty-seven inches from the ceiling at the exact center of the home.

Client Story: The Center Must Hold

My client Julia was at a crossroads in her life. She no longer knew if she wanted to stay with the person she had been with for two decades. She had no space for herself in the midcentury rambler where they resided, and she had recently rented an office just to get some. Much was going well for her. She loved her job, and her kids were doing great, but she felt she was rejecting everything she had chosen, wondering if any of it fit the person she was becoming. She was trying to make room for herself in the home and had plans to paint the exterior colors so they felt more like her.

· Previously, Julia and her husband had moved several walls in their home in order to make it livable for their family, including adding a wall near the center of the home to create the couple's bedroom out of an existing living room. In doing so, they made a small, roughly five-by-nine-foot room at the center of the home, one side of which was a large, two-way brick fireplace. The room had three entrances—one door led to the couple's bedroom, and two arched doorways led to the kitchen and to the children's rooms and a bathroom along a hallway.

The tiny room had become something of a dead zone, a walkthrough; the pets had taken up residence with their crates and litter boxes. In itself, that isn't a problem—pets can bring a fun spark to any space. But this room was more like a closet, and it was also cluttered with a small, overflowing desk and cleaning supplies. And since the light fixture had never been moved to accommodate the new spatial arrangement, it was dark.

My instinct was that this space was fundamental to the family's well-being. Everyone in the family walked through it to reach the rest of the house. As the home's geographic center, the room was asking for messaging that grounded and excited the family and reflected overall harmony. I imagined turning it into a well-lit, sparkling jewel box of sorts, with old wallpaper, new sconces, some portraiture, and so on.

Ultimately, Julia decided she didn't want to take on changing this space or the exterior refresh. After our consult and a few months of reflection, Julia initiated a divorce, they separated amicably, and she found a new place. This happens sometimes: When people begin to change, they notice their spaces don't feel supportive of the person they are becoming and they must make a choice. By becoming conscious of the message embodied in our home's energy, we can become unstuck and proceed with choices that reflect our needs and desires.

FIND YOURSELF

How would you rate the overall well-being of the people who live in your home?

How might you create a visual representation of your spiritual practice for the center of the home?

DESTINY

TAKE your PURPOSE
INTO THE WORLD

23

LEARN HOW TO ASK

Tell me what you want, what you really, really want.

Iconic 1990s song lyrics aside, human desires really do make the world go round, but it helps to dial in what yours are. Now that you know how each section of your home connects to your big-picture aspirations for life, start thinking about how to invite specific, desired outcomes.

Simply by mapping your home and giving a spatial home to areas of your life you have begun the process of articulating for yourself what you want. In a practical way, you made a physical home for the drives that make us feel human. But when it comes to specific desires—such as a raise, a new partner, a better relationship with relatives, a vacation to Bora Bora—you must focus on specific sections and make specific requests. This chapter presents two methods for getting what you want—the reciprocity method, for overall feelings-based goals, and the red-letter method, for goals that can be articulated specifically.

The Reciprocity Method

Carving out physical space for what is important allows us to receive that value in our life. The principle of the reciprocity method is quite simple. It's an idea laid out in every spiritual tradition: We receive whatever we put out into the world.

In practical terms, the reciprocity method inspires agency and action that dances with the energy of change. Whenever I find myself lacking anything in life, my first step is to embody whatever it is that is lacking. When I am lonely, I have a list of five people I always call. When I feel too busy, like I have no time, I look for ways to be generous with my time for others. When I feel unrecognized for my work, I might write Google reviews for businesses I admire. If I don't feel nourished, I might pick up a frozen pot pie from our local pie stand and drop it off at a friend's house. In other words, practice love to receive love. Be generous to experience greater prosperity. Gain influence by admiring others. You may find that what you thought you lacked was what you actually wanted to embody.

Use the reciprocity method when working with the spaces in your home. If you aspire for more of what a certain section on the energy map offers, first embody that. Invite creativity by making space in your life for more creative work. Take the first steps toward travel by hosting people in your home. To increase wealth, look for ways to be generous with the wealth that already exists. For instance, if you have a garden, share those zucchini with abandon! To inspire wisdom, share a great book with a friend.

We often have a skewed idea of what we want. Sometimes, what we need is to experience working toward fulfillment of our desires in order to realize them.

The Red-Letter Method

If you desire something specific, the red-letter method can help shift the energies related to that desire. I use it often with clients and myself, and it's also simple. Just write down, in as much detail as possible, what you would like to happen and express gratefulness for it having already happened. Use a red-ink pen. I like Sharpies, but choose any implement that feels like a joy to use. While some manifesters swear by picking a pen color based on intention, I find the color red always attracts attention, and energy flows where the eye goes.

Why does it work? On the one hand, we are more likely to achieve a goal if it's clearly expressed. Writing does this, while creating a visual cue.[30] Writing encodes what we write in our memory in a more lasting way—as opposed to, say, just thinking about something or saying it out loud. Writing goals down promotes recall and forces us to articulate our desire.

By including gratitude in our letter, this method adds a layer of effectiveness. A growing body of research connects feelings of gratitude to increased overall well-being, even though researchers aren't of one mind as to what gratitude actually is.[31] Are we grateful solely when we receive help, or can we be grateful for states of being? Can we even be grateful for something that hasn't happened yet?

Gratitude is the tail end of hope that has come to fruition. It encompasses what we get, but even more, it honors what we have. As in Marvel movies, there are infinite alternate universes where everything that is possible has happened already. It follows that if you visualize your goals, enshrine them on paper, and show gratitude for them, they will manifest.

Still not convinced? Try it out.

Grab your red pen and get ready to ask for what you want.

1. **Identify what you want:** Be as specific as possible about what you desire to happen. When I say specific, I mean the highest level of specificity you can summon. But don't be unreasonable or explicitly unrealistic. Think of it as you would a goal-setting or strategy session where you imagine actual possibilities that stretch beyond what is already happening in your life.

2. **Express gratitude:** Write that you are thankful for the thing you want as if it has already happened. For example, you might write: "I am so grateful that I was just offered the job I interviewed for at a salary of eighty-five thousand dollars a year."

3. **Place the letter:** Put the note inside a small metal box or wrap it in tinfoil and place it somewhere in the associated energy center in your home. Metal represents clarity of thought and attracts good energy. In practical terms, a note wrapped in metal will be distinguishable from other paper around the room.

4. **Forget about it:** Move on with your life. Don't just sit around waiting for good things to happen. Still work toward your goals in other ways, and trust that the big picture is out of your hands.

Client Story: Moving Stuck Energies

My client Stefania had a boss who just didn't know how to quit. He had actually retired officially—and thrown his own retirement party—and yet, months later, he continued to show up and direct the organization where he had worked for thirty years. Even more disconcerting: He had spoken to multiple people, including Stefania, about them being the chosen person to take over his role. Stefania didn't want his job. She just wanted her boss to retire so he would stop gumming up the works. He was the opposite of a helpful person, and—even worse—he was preventing his coworkers from being people of service in the world.

Stefania lives in a well-kept, midcentury modern home, and I noticed that, on her home energy map, she had what is called a missing corner: the travel and helpful people area was located outside in the garden, near some low raspberry bushes. I had her create the corner by placing a beautiful rock there, and I suggested she write a red letter about how grateful she was that her boss had decided to retire for good. She wrapped the letter in tinfoil and buried it under the rock. After that, the boss never even stepped back in the office. Within a week, he sent an email saying that his work there was done and wished everyone well for their future endeavors—to Stefania's complete elation.

FIND YOURSELF

What is a quality you'd like to receive more of, and how might you embody that quality yourself?

What is something you've been wanting? How might you turn that desire into a specific red letter?

24

KNOW WHEN
TO MOVE ON

O f all of life's major stressors, moving ranks right up there with death, divorce, and new babies. I'm sure there is someone who has packed up a lifetime and discarded what was no longer needed with grace and thoughtfulness, but I have yet to meet that person. For most of us, moving is a fresh hell every time, something we just have to live (and maybe even cry) through to get to the other side. Moving is expensive, it puts our life on hold, and it often comes with a host of emotional imbalances like insomnia, anxiety, and sometimes depression. Is this any surprise, given how connected we are to our spaces? Moving involves a grief process.

Clingy Houses

We don't let go of our spaces lightly, and I suspect they hold on rather tightly to us, too. For instance, a friend of mine had been having a complicated relationship with a historic home where she had lived for over a decade. She had finally started to paint the door and the vestibule as part of a larger exterior paint project, and right then, the housing market shifted dramatically. Suddenly, her home was worth more than she ever imagined, and there was another home on the market that fit her family's needs better. She quickly prepared the home for sale, and her offer was accepted on the new house.

Except that her old house didn't want her to go! My friend had two offers fall through on her old house while she waited to buy her new one, leaving me to suspect that her old home wasn't yet ready for her to move. I suggested that she write a letter to her old home, letting it know how thankful she was for the role it had played in her life, and how she knew that the next family would love and need the home just as much, if not more. Her home sold promptly thereafter, and my friend was free.

Making the Decision: Move or Renovate

How do you know when you're ready to move on? Many people move to have more space and better amenities, or to live closer to a job or in a more vibrant community, but according to the US Census Bureau, the main reason people move is to be near family. So if you're happy in the location where you live, the real question is: When you notice that your spatial needs have changed, is it better to address them with a move or to renovate?

In recent years, I love how many families are drawing inspiration from home renovation shows and choosing to improve their homes. So many of these homeowners are attached to their home and their neighborhoods, and they prefer to take on the stresses of renovation rather than relocation. The result, I've noticed, is more vibrant, safer, tighter-knit communities, which adds to the well-being of everyone. To me, choosing to stay and love on the spaces we have is a symbolic gesture of loving our own choices and valuing interconnectedness over consumption.

That said, the old model of home ownership holds that you should never remodel your home beyond what the market will bear, so that you get your investment back when it's time to sell. Kitchen and bathroom remodels tend to hold their value the most over time, but that custom basement bowling alley? Probably not.

Consider moving if some or all of these apply:

- Your family has grown and you absolutely need more space.
- You desire a major upgrade in lifestyle.
- You aren't particularly attached to your community.
- You find yourself battling your home's spatial configuration on a daily basis.
- Your long-term goals have changed.
- You aren't using the spaces you have.
- Your current cost of living has become untenable.
- Opportunity is calling you elsewhere.

Consider renovating if some or all of these apply:

- You love your neighborhood and your neighbors.
- Your kids need to stay in the same school district.
- Your memories in the home outweigh your urge for a lifestyle upgrade.
- You have the budget for major upgrades.
- The market is tight and there aren't many other homes for sale.
- You have a work-from-home job.
- You are aging and the specific home adjustments you need can occur in your existing home.
- The home you have could work better with some tweaks.

Don't Ghost Your Own House

It's bad form to leave a party without saying goodbye, and the same etiquette holds true with any space you inhabit. Never ghost your own house. Moving spaces calls for a personalized ceremony, so conduct whatever ritual signals to your spirit and your home's spirit that the time to move on has come. Writing a letter always works, but I have found that taking a moment to say goodbye to the home suffices.

Here is how I suggest leaving a space:

- Stand in the geographic center of the home.
- Thank the home for everything it has given you.
- Let your immediate memories of the home wash through you like the world's fastest film montage.
- Tell the home you are moving on and that it will be cared for.

Carry Your Purpose with You

Just this past year, I said goodbye to my childhood home, the one we returned to after all of those open house visits we did when I was a child, the house my mother never moved out of despite looking for other options for forty years. I hadn't lived in the home for two decades, so I had already shifted my own concept of home to the one where I live with my family, but it was a dazzling emotional experience nonetheless. I had recently convinced my mother to move across the country to live near us, and after just ten years of prodding, she was ready. I'm not in the habit of telling my mother what to do—as a proud inheritor of her single-mindedness, I get how much she needs to be self-directed—but

I told her to talk to her house and let it know she was moving on. Did she do it? I have no idea. I'm guessing no. That's between her and her house. But the house sold in three days, and she was able to get the entire process completed in about six months.

On my last day there after helping to clean out a lifetime's worth of stuff, with my mom waiting in the car, the engine running, I snuck back to the kitchen, in the center of the home, and spoke to the place that had rooted me, made me a creative, provided me peace, and taken care of the most important woman in my life. Though I had to return home before the movers came, I felt a strong urge to make these next few weeks of upheaval feel less torturous for her. So I gathered myself.

"I'm taking her," I said. "Thank you for all you have done for her, but I'm going to take care of her now. You can let go."

Love Your Home

It really doesn't matter what metaphor we use to talk about home—memory palace, command central, the center of the world, creativity den, oracle. Your home has the power to be a great collaborator in your life, and it deserves as much love as you do. Talk to your home. Let it know what you want and let it send you messages for how to get there. Attend to your energy at home with the understanding that the world needs you to be safe and comfortable but also aligned and purposeful. Forget the things you can't change and redecorate what you can. Be open to the surprises that come with living a human life. Dance with the energies of your space. Treat your home like the powerful energy vortex it is and you'll never lack for magic or meaning.

RESOURCES

$ = Affordable $$ = Midrange $$$ = High-end

Animal Décor

Jonathan Adler $$$
jonathanadler.com
The famous potter-turned-décor-icon's animal sculptures are at home in modern and traditional spaces.

Chairish $$
chairish.com
This curated site for rare, vintage, and contemporary décor is a trove for animal objects and much more.

Sound Clearing

Space Clearing $$$
spaceclearing.com
The original space-clearing expert Karen Kingston sells authentic hand-forged bells from Bali.

Himalayas Shop $$
himalayasshop.com
Hand-hammered singing bowls from Nepal make great space-clearing tools and provide an income for Indigenous craftspeople.

Busts

The Ancient Home $$$
etsy.com/shop/TheAncientHome
This leading European online retailer of busts from antiquity and recent history also has décor inspired by ancient life.

Museum Shop Italy $$$
museum-shop.it
A purveyor of museum-quality marble and bronze busts and sculptures with a focus on ancient Roman and Greek statuary, this site also has some modern, colored versions.

Senan's Art Shop $
etsy.com/shop/SenansArtShop
This source for 3D printed busts on Etsy has a high likelihood of having your favorite figure from antiquity at a reasonable price.

Candles

Anecdote Candles $
anecdotecandles.com
Playful statement candles—one is called Flannel and Fedoras—also pair great essences by natural perfumers.

The Magical Bee $$

themagicalbee.com

This purveyor's candles—some with crystals—emit a sweet glow and well-balanced aromas in a completely nontoxic base of soy, coconut, and beeswax.

Crystals

Energy Muse $

energymuse.com

Heather Askinosie, the author of the well-received manual *Crystal365*, created this source for well-priced crystal clusters, points, and jewelry.

Sage Crystals $

sagecrystals.com

This source allows you to connect with crystals by astrological sign, chakra, and color, and it also sells crystal décor.

Moonrise Crystals $

moonrisecrystals.com

Ethically sourced crystals from this company are tracked from mine to consumer, ensuring they have more of their specific energies intact.

Hardware

Rejuvenation $$$

rejuvenation.com

Rejuvenation sells American-made hardware that leans from traditional to modern and everything in between.

Schoolhouse $$$

schoolhouse.com

This store's classically modern American-made hardware is a favorite of designers.

The Nanz Company $$$

nanz.com

This American purveyor has over three thousand products from historic to modern with a variety of finishes, including highly engineered hinges and locks.

Bath Soaks and Tub Teas

Aquarian Soul $

shopaquariansoul.com

The original crystal-infused apothecary makes its own bath teas and soaks for use alongside bath crystals and bathing stones.

Moon Bath $

moonbath.com

These products for use alongside the lunar calendar combine Ayurvedic practices with modern bathing rituals.

Seagrape Apothecary $

seagrapeapothecary.com

Self-care products from this woman-owned purveyor are part magic and all pleasure.

Palo Santo

Bursera $$

bursera.com

This company provides sustainably sourced palo santo in various modalities, like sticks, incense, and oil.

Floracopeia $$

floracopeia.com

The original purveyors of sustainable palo santo are a treasured resource for bringing the wisdom of scent into your life.

MIZU $$

mizubrand.com

Maker of a full palo santo gift set—burn wood, candle, and fragrance—this botanical perfumer does scent right.

Sacred Wood Essence $

sacredwoodessence.com

This sustainable source of palo santo pays fair prices to producers and replenishes harvested trees.

House Plants and Plant Accessories

EcoVibe $$

ecovibestyle.com

A Black-owned sustainable-style outpost in Portland with a stellar houseplant operation.

Pistils Nursery $$

pistilsnursery.com

This Portland resource sells rare and unusual plants, pottery, and products for houseplant mamas and papas.

Potted $$$

pottedstore.com

Outdoor furniture, a wide range of pot options, and a gorgeous array of houseplants defines this go-to LA source.

Ritual Salt

LA Salt Co. $$

lasaltco.com

These pure and blended self-care salts hail from a family operation in Los Angeles.

Saltworks $

seasalt.com

Headquartered in Woodinville, Washington, this trusted source sells premium-grade specialty salts, including Dead Sea salt.

Natural Cleaning Supplies

The Earthling Co. $
theearthlingco.com
These gorgeous products elevate
the home while treading lightly
on the earth.

Earth Hero $
earthhero.com
Entire green lifestyles can be built
by getting to know this source for
sustainable products.

Grove Collaborative $
grove.co
This large-scale site is a go-to for
easy-to-order and reorder green home
products.

Texture-Rich Home Goods

Jungalow $$
jungalow.com
The home of designer Justina Blakeney
has oodles of texture, story-rich home
products, animal décor, and an elevated
global aesthetic.

MINNA $$$
minna-goods.com
This queer-led business sources ethically
made artisan textiles for the home from
around the world.

Swahili Modern $$$
swahilimodern.com
An importer of African goods, this
company sources products fairly and
stays atop current styles.

Wallpaper

Cole & Son $$
cole-and-son.com
This storied British producer runs the
gamut from textured and simple to
geometric, botanical, historical, and
whimsical.

Graham & Brown $$
grahambrown.com
A longtime creator of wallpapers in many
styles, Graham & Brown also designs
fetching botanical wall murals.

House of Hackney $$$
houseofhackney.com
A favorite British purveyor, Hackney
makes high-vibe, maximalist wallpapers.

NOTES

1. Kendra Cherry, "The Color Psychology of Blue," Very Well Mind, February 21, 2020, https://www.verywellmind.com/the-color-psychology-of-blue-2795815.

2. Ezequiel Morsella et al., "Homing In on Consciousness in the Nervous System: An Action-Based Synthesis," *Behavioral and Brain Sciences* 39 (2016), https://www.cambridge.org/core/journals/behavioral-and-brain-sciences/article/homing-in-on-consciousness-in-the-nervous-system-an-actionbased-synthesis/2483CA8F40A087A0A7AAABD40E0D89B2.

3. Sy Adler and Mark Bello, "Banning the 'Snout House': The Politics of Design in Portland, Oregon," *Journal of Architectural and Planning Research* 21:3 (Autumn 2004), https://www.jstor.org/stable/43031076.

4. Gino Francesco and Michael I. Norton, "Why Rituals Work," *Scientific American*, May 14, 2013, https://www.scientificamerican.com/article/why-rituals-work/.

5. Adrian L. Lopresti, "Salvia (Sage): A Review of Its Potential Cognitive-Enhancing and Protective Effects," *Drugs in R&D* 17, no. 1 (March 2017), https://www.ncbi.nlm.nih.gov/pmc/articles/PMC5318325.

6. Teresa M. Kutchma, "The Effects of Room Color on Stress Perception: Red Versus Green Environments," *The Journal of Undergraduate Research at Minnesota State University, Mankato* 3, no. 3 (2003), https://cornerstone.lib.mnsu.edu/jur/vol3/iss1/3.

7. Nurlelawati Ab. Jalil, Rodzyah Mohd Yunus, and Normahdia S. Said, "Environmental Colour Impact on Human Behavior: A Review," *Procedia Social and Behavioral Sciences* 35 (2012), https://www.sciencedirect.com/science/article/pii/S1877042812003746.

8. Jalil, "Environmental Colour Impact."

9. Wade T. Lijewski, "Integrating Environmental Psychology to Benefit Your Clients," *Elite Learning*, July 12, 2022, http://orthomolecular.org/library/jom/1988/pdf/1988-v03n04-p202.pdf.

10. Aleksandra Ćurčić et al., "Effects of Color in Interior Design," Seventh International Conference, Contemporary Achievements in Civil Engineering (Serbia), April 2019, https://www.researchgate.net/publication/333928432_Effects_of_color_in_interior_design.

11. Ćurčić, "Effects of Color."

12. Sibila Marques and Maria Luisá Lima, "Living in Grey Areas: Industrial Activity and Psychological Health," *Journal of Environmental Psychology* 31, no. 4 (December 2011), https://www.researchgate.net/publication/228094917_Living_in_grey_areas_Industrial_activity_and_psychological_health.

13. Jalil, "Environmental Colour Impact."

14. Cecilia Rios Velasco, "Color and Visual Comfort," University of Texas at Austin, School of Architecture, accessed on May 28, 2022, https://www.scribd.com/document/436724119/Color-and-visual-comfort.

15. Sabine Kastner, "Attention, Please!," *Nature Neuroscience* 4 (October 2001), https://www.nature.com/articles/nn1001-971.

16. Sandra C. Matz, Joe J. Gladstone, and David Stillwell, "Money Buys Happiness When Spending Fits Our Personality," *Association for Psychological Science* 27, no. 5 (2016), https://journals.sagepub.com/doi/abs/10.1177/0956797616635200.

17. Sophie Fessl, "How Our Brains Respond to Texture," Dana Foundation, May 22, 2019, https://www.dana.org/article/how-our-brains-respond-to-texture.

18. Marina Iosifyan and Olga Korolkova, "Emotions Associated with Different Textures During Touch," *Consciousness and Cognition* 71, no. 1 (April 2019), https://www.researchgate.net/publication/332564189_Emotions_associated_with_different_textures_during_touch.

19. Dan King and Chris Janiszewski, "Affect-Gating," *Journal of Consumer Research* 38, no. 4 (December 1, 2011), https://academic.oup.com/jcr/article-abstract/38/4/697/1859028.

20. Chong Wang et al., "Effect of Wall Texture on Perceptual Spaciousness of Indoor Space," *International Journal of Environmental Research and Public Health* 17, no. 11 (June 2020), https://www.ncbi.nlm.nih.gov/pmc/articles/PMC7312763.

21. Mohamed Boubekri et al., "Impact of Windows and Daylight Exposure on Overall Health and Sleep Quality of Office Workers: A Case-Control Pilot Study," *Journal of Clinical Sleep Medicine* 10, no. 6 (June 15, 2014), https://www.ncbi.nlm.nih.gov/pmc/articles/PMC4031400.

22. Michael Slepian and Max Weisbuch, "Shedding Light on Insight: Priming Bright Ideas," *Journal of Experimental Social Psychology* 46, no. 4 (July 1, 2010), https://www.ncbi.nlm.nih.gov/pmc/articles/PMC2905814.

23. Ximena Garcia-Rada, Ovul Sezer, and Michael Norton, "Rituals and Nuptials: The Emotional and Relational Consequences of Relationship Rituals," *Journal of the Association for Consumer Research* 4, no. 2 (April 2019), https://www.hbs.edu/faculty/Pages/item.aspx?num=55865.

24. University of Exeter, "Designing Your Own Workspace Improves Health, Happiness, and Productivity," *ScienceDaily*, September 8, 2010, https://www.sciencedaily.com/releases/2010/09/100907104035.htm.

25. Donald Rattner, *My Creative Space: How to Design Your Home to Stimulate Ideas and Spark Innovation* (New York: Skyhorse, 2019), 37.

26. Christopher D. Lynn, "Hearth and Campfire Influences on Arterial Blood

Pressure: Defraying the Costs of the Social Brain through Fireside Relaxation," *Evolutionary Psychology* 12, no. 5 (April 2014), https://journals.sagepub.com/doi/full/10.1177/147470491401200509.

27. Eric Jaffe, "Why Our Brains Love Curvy Architecture," *Fast Company*, October 17, 2013, https://www.fastcompany.com/3020075/why-our-brains-love-curvy-architecture.

28. "How Looking at Art Can Help Your Brain," University of Arizona Global Campus, December 9, 2021, https://www.uagc.edu/blog/how-looking-at-art-can-help-your-brain.

29. Sean Joyner, "The Psychology of High Ceilings and Creative Work Spaces," Archinet, April 15, 2020, https://archinect.com/features/article/150193563/the-psychology-of-high-ceilings-and-creative-work-spaces.

30. Mark Murphy, "Neuroscience Explains Why You Need to Write Down Your Goals If You Actually Want to Achieve Them," *Forbes*, April 15, 2018, https://www.forbes.com/sites/markmurphy/2018/04/15/neuroscience-explains-why-you-need-to-write-down-your-goals-if-you-actually-want-to-achieve-them/?sh=1409ac187905.

31. Alex M. Wood, Jeffrey J. Froh, and Adam W. A. Geraghty, "Gratitude and Well-Being: A Review and Theoretical Integration," *Clinical Psychology Review* 30, no. 7 (March 2010), https://www.researchgate.net/publication/44581429_Gratitude_and_well-being_A_review_and_theoretical_integration.

ACKNOWLEDGMENTS

I got really lucky. I have dreamed of book-making for my entire life and could not have asked for a better group of collaborators for this one. I have the best agent, Stacey Glick, and the most thoughtful, talented, and kind editor in Cara Bedick. The whole team at Prism has made this process the best kind of fun: Thank you to Lynn Grady, Michelle Triant, Liz Anderson, Cecilia Santini, Reg Lim, Pamela Geismar, and Yuhong Guo. Thank you for seeing what this idea could become and for being an immediate "hell, yes!"

I'm immensely grateful to illustrator Mar Hernández, whose work adds magic, mystery, and charm to everything she touches. Mar, the more I engage with your work, the more it moves me to see endless imaginative possibilities in every idea.

To my mother, Susan Buchheit Grosvenor—family grand dame and my companion on so many house tours—thank you for giving me the filter of my own taste and the compass of experience to guide me. We don't get to choose our parents, but if I could, I would always pick you.

Thanks to my sister, Dr. Ashley Tian, who shares with me her zest for elsewhere—here's to more trips to high-vibe places.

Mary Adams, thank you for always sharing in my delight in a life of books. No one has been more excited for me than you have been.

Samantha Rynearson, our friendship transcends space and time.

A special feeling of gratitude gathers in me when I think of the friends and family whose presence and help have made this book possible, especially: Ken Rynearson, Jill Mann, Tai James, Sinell Harney, Amy Scholer, Karen and John Olson, Kate and Travis Bonilla, Maria Stuart, Jenn Williams, Kate Brown, Jamie Howe, Dominique Bjorlin, Gabi Hinoveanu, Amber Rae Bridges, and Melissa and Andrew Ranks.

My deepest gratitude extends to my friend Stephanie Lenox for helping me outline my ideas in the early stages of writing and for sending me all the prizes I unlocked along the way. If I could, I would install you in my office as director of my chorus of muses.

I am grateful to the following writing mentors who saw me in their classrooms and shaped how I see the world: Stephen Bloom, Claire Dederer, Don McLeese, Paul Kellermann, and Ralf Saborrosch, all of whom saw something in me worth cultivating.

I also thank people on my health team who were part of the recovery that happened alongside this book: James Carter, Molly Weinbender, and Kira Shurtz.

My space gets remade every time I encounter the works of designers Jessica Helgerson, Emily Henderson, Beata Heuman, Justina Blakeney, and Lauren Liess. And I continue to be indebted to my feng shui mentors Cheryl Janis, who first sent me down the path of shaping home energies, and Terah Kathryn Collins, who showed me how to make it a life pursuit.

All of the learning, play, intentions, adjustments, and love that go into making a home would be for nothing without the people who share our tiny world: our sons Dash and Griffin. You are limitless joy.

And to my husband, Adam—again, and again, and again.

ABOUT THE AUTHOR

Emily Grosvenor is a design writer, magazine editor, and home consultant who helps people align their spaces with their goals for their lives. She is a certified feng shui consultant, a former Fulbright scholar, and creator of the global holiday World Tessellation Day. Emily lives in a wine country town just outside of Portland, Oregon, with her husband and two sons.